THE TREATMENT OF NATURE IN GERMAN LITERATURE FROM GÜNTHER TO THE APPEARANCE OF GOETHE'S WERTHER

THE TREATMENT OF NATURE IN GERMAN LITERATURE FROM GÜNTHER TO THE APPEARANCE OF GOETHE'S WERTHER

BY
MAX BATT

KENNIKAT PRESS
Port Washington, N. Y./London

THE TREATMENT OF NATURE IN GERMAN LITERATURE
FROM GUNTHER TO THE APPEARANCE OF GOETHE'S WERTHER

First published 1902
Reissued in 1969 by Kennikat Press
Library of Congress Catalog Card No: 72-91034
SBN 8046-0644-7

Manufactured by Taylor Publishing Company   Dallas, Texas

INTRODUCTION.

EVEN a cursory examination of the carefully compiled and exceptionally well-annotated bibliographies of Biese (Zeitschrift für vergleichende Literaturgeschichte, VII, 311 ff., and XI, 211 ff.) and von Klenze (Journal of Germanic Philology, II, 243 ff.) will reveal to one unfamiliar with the general theme of the treatment of nature in literature and art the increasing interest manifested of late in this subject. Since the publication of Biese's fundamental work, *Die Entwickelung des Naturgefühls im Mittelalter und in der Neuzeit* (1888), there is, however, less need of suggestive studies covering the whole field — as F. T. Palgrave attempted to do in *Landscape and Poetry* (1897) — than of detailed investigations of single periods, like Miss Reynolds's *The Treatment of Nature in English Poetry between Pope and Wordsworth* (1896). The (approximately) corresponding period in German literature — that is, the half-century before Goethe — has, to my knowledge, been discussed, outside of Biese's suggestive rather than exhaustive chapter dealing with the poetry, only in a "Programm" by Winter, *Beiträge zur Geschichte des Naturgefühls* (Harburg, 1883). As Winter had to reduce his investigation to a very narrow compass, he could accord only a more or less summary treatment to the principal authors of the period, and did not go beyond the realm of poetry for data pertaining to the nature-sense. The present study is an attempt, not only to enlarge upon his discussion of nature in the poetry between Günther and the young Goethe, but also to discover to some extent in the letters, travels, and fiction of the period what indications there are of the development of the nature-sense in the second and third quarters of the eighteenth century. I have resorted to the illustrations found in Winter's and Biese's investigations only when some special reason induced me to use them. Furthermore, as the time limit of my study is the year 1774, I have endeavored not to discuss any works after this date, unless they are of prime importance in the immediate development of the nature-sense, as in the case of Stolberg and Goethe.

I.

THE TREATMENT OF NATURE IN THE SEVENTEENTH CENTURY.

To UNDERSTAND more fully the change of attitude toward nature which came to pass in the eighteenth century, endeavor should be made to find out the chief characteristics that marked the treatment of nature in the poetry of the seventeenth century. For this purpose it is perhaps best to examine in detail the works of some representative poet and draw illustrations from others indicative of the same spirit. Martin Opitz (1597–1639) is, no doubt, the central figure of the period under discussion. His own as well as succeeding generations looked upon him as their fountain-head; hence his view of nature is probably typical of the seventeenth century. It may be noted at once that he refers not infrequently to idyllic life — he was, as is well known, influenced particularly by Horace — and that a strikingly large number of his similes and apostrophes appertain to the life in nature. Pure descriptions, on the other hand, are of rare occurrence.

Beginning may be made by noting his references to morning, day, and night. The poet bids the hours to hasten and the dawn to harness Phœbus's horses, and inquires of the moon why she tarries — all this because of the absence of his beloved.[1] He calls upon Aurora to put on her red and yellow dress and shine forth, so that the pearly dew may no longer moisten the fields and the mist of the clouds be dispersed; for the entire earth, mountain, and valley should enjoy this feast (namely birthday).[2]

The sun, the eye of the world,[3] the ornament of this earth, is implored

[1] *Vom Abwesen seiner Liebsten*, 5.

[2] *Geburtsgetichte*, 4.—For references to morning in the works of other seventeenth-century writers see Anselm von Ziegler, *Asiatische Banise*, 344, 372, 432: "Die morgenröthe gläntzt mit lichten rosen-haaren. . . . . Mit der verschwundnen nacht schläft das gestirne ein. Die nachtigal erwacht, und will beschäfftigt seyn, Das neue tageslicht aufs schönste zu begrüssen."—Simon Dach, *Morgen-Lied*, 96, and especially Friedrich Spee, *Trutz-Nachtigall*, 1: "Wann Morgenröt sich zieret Mit zartem Rosen-glanz, Und gar sich dann verlieret Der nächtlich Sternentanz; Gleich lüstet mich spazieren In grünen Lorbeerwald. . . . . Der grüne Wald ertönet Von krausem Vogelsang, Mit Stauden stolz gekrönet Die Kruften geben Klang, Die Bächlein krumb geflochten Auch lieblich stimmen ein, Von Steinlein ange-fochten Gar süsslich sausen drein."—Other passages in the *Trutz-Nachtigall* (34, 54, 73, 77) show Spee's fondness for morning walks, while still others make mention of the beauty of the dewdrops (87, 137).

[3] P. 109.

by Judith[1] not to be angry because of her going to the enemy of God. In another place[2] the lovely beams of the sun, which gleamed from the peaks of the mountains, seemed to console, as it were, the speaker. When the old woman (*Schäfferey*) pronounced the incantation, the sun seemed to grow pale with fright, no singing of birds was heard, nothing stirred but the trembling trees.[3] The poet asks, "What is more beautiful than women ?" and answers, "Not the flowers in the fields, nor the land and the wide sea, when they are painted by the beams of the sun coming from Ethiopia."[4]

Evening receives more consideration. Observe this description : "Wie schöne sieht es auss, Wann nun der Abendstern dess Himmels blaue Hauss Mit seinem Lichte ziert, wirfft von der Berge Spitzen Den Schatten in den Fluss, an dem die Vögel sitzen Und singen überlaut ? Es scheint der Wald folgt nach, Gleich wie das Wasser scheusst, und schwimmet in der Bach."[5] Descriptions somewhat different are found in the poems *Elegie* and *Auff Herrn Johann Seylers Hochzeit*.[6] Although night brings peace and rest to all, for the poet it is a sorrowful time, if the two stars (the eyes of his beloved) do not shine upon him.[7]

The moon, whose light irradiates the brown night, and the stars, whose luster paints the structure of the sky, are asked by Holofernes (*Judith*, 331) to appear joyful.[8]

---

[1] *Judith*, 328 : "Sonne, Zier der Erde, Die du zu der Nachtruh schreitest Und die müden Pferde In die See zum Trincken reitest. . . . ."—Cf. Andreas Gryphius, *Cardenio und Celinde*, l. 624 : "Wie kan ich sonder Grauen Das Auge dieser Welt, die lichte Sonn anschaun, Die vorhin meine Freud, ietzt meine Schmach bestrahlt Und mein bestürtzt Gesicht mit scheuer Röthe mahlt ?"

[2] *Schäfferey von der Nimfen Hercinie*, 108.   [3] P. 136.

[4] *An Herrn David Müllern*, über die Geburt seiner lieben Tochter, 33. Note also this simile: "die Schönheit des Leibes (ist) ein Heroldt der Tugend . . . . als wie der Glantz, welcher sich diesen Morgen von hiesigem Gefilde blicken liess, eine Vorbote der güldenen Sonnen war" (*Schäfferey*, 114).

[5] *Zlatna*, 49.—Cf. Lohenstein, *Cleopatra* (l. 1370): "Wie wenn der düstre Schimmer Dess braunen Abends itzt die blauen Hügel deckt . . . ,," and (l. 2815): "Doch wie die Abendt-Röth, Indem sie in das Meer bepurpert untergeht, Ein helles Morgen-Licht der Sonnen uns bedeutet. . . . ."

[6] "Die Sonn' hat sich verkrochen, Der Tag ist gantz dahin, Der Mond ist angebrochen, Die Arbeit-Trösterin, Die Nacht, hat angeleget Ihr schwartzes Trauerkleyd, Kein Grass ist das sich reget, Kein Baum nicht weit und breit. Die Welt ist schon zu Bette, Und hat die Augen zu, Wir schlaffen in die Wette, Das Meer liegt auch in Ruh ; Nur zweene Geister wachen, Der Krieg- und Liebesgott" (37).

[7] P. 17, and *Nachtklage*, 10.—Andreas Gryphius, *Leo Arminius*, Reyen der Priester, 58, 93, and *Cardenio und Celinde* (l. 1710): "Die dunckel-braune Nacht Hatt' in den Mittel-punct des Himmels sich gemacht; Diane stieg hervor mit halb-verwandten Wangen . . . ."—Simon Dach, 32: "Die Sonne lest des Himmels Saal, Versetzt mit Sternen ohne Zahl, Wie einen bunten Teppich stehen, Der Schlaf trit Wald und Städten zu, Gönnt Vieh und Menschen ihre Ruh!"

[8] Cardenio (Gryphius, *Cardenio und Celinde*, ll. 1140 ff.) implores the stars to assist him, and in describing the quiet of the night he says : "Man hört von weitem nur der wackern Hunde Heulen Und einsames Geschrey der ungeparten Eulen."—Spee (XIII, 63) asks the moon and stars to mourn with him.

Spring is the only season which the poet describes.[1] All its striking features are narrated in the dialogue between Nuszler, Venater, and Buchner in the *Schäfferey* (139) :

N. Wann alles überschneyt Und zugewintert ist, so kompt der Frühling wieder.

V. Dann hört man durch die Lufft der Vögel schöne Lieder.

B. Das Vieh verlest den Stall.

N. Die Weide wird verjüngt.

V. Die Blumen finden sich.

B. Cibelens Fichte bringt Ein neues Laub herfür.

N. Die fromme Birke blühet.

V. Die Eiche schlaget auss.

B. Der süsse Weinstock siehet Sich nach den Augen umb.

N. Der Obstbaum zeucht sein Kleidt, Die Blätter wieder an.

V. Das Stadtvolk ist erfreut.

B. Das Dorff geht auf das Feldt.

N. So last uns dem vertrauen, Der Dorff, Statt, Obst und Wein, der Bäume, Feldt und Auen, Der Vieh und Vögel hegt; Sein werther Sonnenschein wird nach der strengen Lufft uns desto lieber seyn. . . . .

This gives us, not an original picture, to be sure, but a typical description of the arrival of spring by seventeenth-century poets in Germany.

Other phenomena of the sky which are mentioned are the wind, thunderstorm, and lightning. The power of the first Opitz recognizes full well, for he says : ". . . . es ist nichts auff der Welt, Das fast dess Windes Macht die rechte Wage hält, Weil auch die höchste Krafft ohn ihn sich nicht beweget. Der Wind macht einig nur, dass sich das Feuer reget, Ohn ihn entschläft die See." [2] Continuing, the poet compares the fire of the volcano to the action of the winds : "So

---

[1] This is true of the poets of the seventeenth century, with some exceptions, however. Dach (*Herbst-Liedchen*, 107, 136) speaks of the sadness of autumn, and Spee (81) of the fertility of summer. These two poets have, also, together with Logau, characterized spring and the month of May in a manner less conventional than is usually found in the works of their contemporaries. The following lines are especially remarkable : " Dieser Monat [Mai] ist ein Kuss, den der Himmel gibt der Erde, Dass sie ietzund seine Braut, künfftig eine Mutter werde" (Logau, 173). — " Diese Meyen-Zeit, Da sich Himmel, See und Land knüpffen in ein Heyrath-Band . . . . Hört man in den Wäldern nicht, Wie sich Baum und Baum bespricht?" (Dach, 120). — " Der trübe Winter ist fürbei, Die Kranich wiederkehren, Nun reget sich der Vogelschrei, Die Nester sich vermehren " (Spee, 26). — Grimmelshausen says (XXXIV, 106): " [Simplicius geht] . . . . die Donau hinauf nacher Ulm . . . . weil es eben im Mai und lustig zu reisen war." — Other references to spring are found in Dach, *Vor Jahrs Liedchen*, 114; *Vorjahrs-Lied*, 119; *Auf Reinnar Leos Hochzeit*, 129; Spee, 70; David Schirmer, 374; Georg Harsdörffer, *Der Frühling;* and Philipp von Zesen, *An seine Gedanken bei herzunahenden Frühling.*

[2] *Vesuvius*, 155.

geht das Feuer an wie etwan von den Winden, Wann ihr ergrimmter
Sturmb den Wald zusammen treibt, Ein Baum so offt und viel dess
andern Aeste reibt, Dass durch Erhitzung sich der liechte Loh
empöret, Von dem zu wüten wird nicht eher auffgehöret, Biss mit der
Püsche Zier den Stämmen auch das Kleid Der Erden Laub und
Grass, durchauss ist abgemeyt." A thunderstorm is thus pictured:
"Das Liecht ward schwartze Nacht, der Himmel lieff zusammen, In
dickes Finsterniss, die Wolcken gaben Flammen Und eilten hefftig
fort, man sahe keinen Tag, Als wann der grimme Plitz durch einen
Donnerschlag Vorher gesendet kam, der Winde starckes Prausen
Bewegte Wald und Berg mit seinem wilden Sausen, Die Lufft ward
lauter See, der Höllen gantzes Reich Erregte seine Krafft, die Bäume
wurden bleich."[1]

It was stated in the first paragraph of this chapter that nature was
used almost exclusively in comparisons. Particularly is this true of all
sea-pictures. Although the similes and metaphors which may be noted
show no great originality, yet it is worthy of note that so many (four-
teen) are drawn from this feature in nature. The god of war,[2] says the
poet, chases hither and thither, like the furious sea, when the troubled
waters climb up to the clouds and the waves drive one another toward
the shore, rapidly and in countless numbers. The turbulence of the
sea, its horrors and dangers, are pointed out frequently, and Opitz himself is the author of the following lines, which are most characteristic
of the general attitude toward nature, as it is found expressed in the
writings of the representative men of the age:

> Auff grosser See sind grosse Wellen,
> Viel Klippen, Sturm und harter Wind;
> Wer klug ist, bleibet bey den Quellen,
> Die in den grünen Wäldern sind.[3]

The features of his inland scenery are the brook, the hill and

---

[1] *Schäfferey*, etc., 137.   [2] *Lob des Krieges-Gottes*, 93.

[3] P. 16. Cf. *Vielgut*, 99; *Trostgedichte in Widerwertigkeit dess Krieges*, 271, 318, and especially
312; *Judith*, 331.— Cf. also Anselm von Ziegler, *Asiatische Banise*, 382: "Die feste liebe bleibt, wenn
schon die stolze see Den grund-erbosten schaum biss an die sterne schmeisset, Und segel, mast und baum
in saltz und wasser reisset." — Lohenstein, *Arminius und Thusnelda:* "Liebe, Furcht, Hoffnung,
Eyversucht, Rache und Verzweiflung machten in seinem Hertzen ein schrecklicher Ungewitter, als ein
Ocean auf der See seyn kan, wo ein rasender Wind wider den andern stösst, eine Welle die andere verschlingt, der Blitz die stockfinstere Nacht erleuchtet, vom Donner Wolcken und Schiffe zerbersten, Himmel und Erde sich mit einander vermischen." — Spee, *Trutz-Nachtigall*, iii, 83: "Das wilde Meer
nun brauset Und wüthet ungestüm, Nun still es wieder sauset Und liegt in runder Krüm." — Fleming, 64:
"Das böse Meer, das heute brauset, Wird morgen still und milder sein. Wenn Boreas hat ausgesauset,
so tritt ein linder Zephyr ein."

valley, and the forest. It is to the last that the poet resorts when seeking rest.[1] In a pastoral mood he sings:

> So weit die grüne Lust unfl hohen Wälder gehn,
> So weit wird mein Gedicht' an allen Bäumen stehn.
> Ihr Oerter voller Freud', ihr Auffenthalt der Hirten,
> Ihr Bäch', ihr Ahornbäum', ihr Quell, ihr zarten Myrten,
> Ihr Thäler, ihr Gebirg', ihr Blumen und ihr Stein',
> Ihr Wohnhaus aller Rhu, bey euch wüntsch ich zu seyn.[2]

His joy in nature he expresses thus: "Ist nicht der schöne Bau der Erden das Gemach Und stoltze Haus für uns, der Himmel unser Dach, Das grüne Feld ein Saal, mit Bäumen schön umbringet? Ist nicht die volle See, die reichlich Speise bringet, Die Brunnen klaren Tranck?"[3] A semi-circular valley, full of brooks, hamlets, farm-houses, and sheepfolds,[4] and inclosed in the distance by gradually rising hills — such is his favorite prospect.[5]

We should observe, too, the frequent recurrence of one feature of the landscape, which is quite common to many poets of this age and of the following age, the spring or brook. This he apostrophizes in several poems. *Ueber den Queckbrunnen zum Buntzlau in Schlesien* he says:

---

[1] Cf. Dafne, 69: "Wer sein gutes Leben Will der freyen Ruh ergeben, Reisst sich von der argen Last, Suchet für das süsse Leyden Felder, Wild, Gepüsch und Heyden. Cf. p. 13, note 3.— Cf. also Andreas Gryphius, *Straff-Gedicht*, 375: "Man fragt, woher es doch sey kommen, ... Dass mich ein rauher Wald ergetzt." — *Leo Arminius*, 58: "O selig . . . . der nur die Wälder kennt, In welchen er ernährt, der keine Diener nennt. . . . ." — Anselm von Ziegler, *Asiatische Banise*, 65, 424: "Ihr schönen tannen ihr! ihr holden wälderriesen! . . . . Ihr seyd von dem, was sonst die seelen quält, befreyt. . . . . Beliebte einsamkeit! indem die sorgen schwinden, So kan mein hertze mehr vergnügung bey dir finden als in der Perser burg." — Lohenstein (*Cleopatra*, l. 3327): "Wie selig sind, die den Schmaragd der Auen Für der Päläste Gold erwehlen! . . . ." — Dach, *Vorjahrs Liedchen*, 124: "Die Lust hat mich gezwungen Zu fahren in den Wald, Wo durch der Vögel Zungen Die gantze Luft erschallt. . . . ." — Heinrich Mühlpfort, 346: "Ein Pusch, ein frischer Brunnen, ein blühendes Gesträuche, Schafft mir mehr Freud' und Wonn', als wenn in Venus Reiche Der liebe Natur (Nectar?) quillt."

[2] *Dass die Poeterey unsterblich sey*, 14.   [3] *Trostgedicht*, 297.

[4] *Schäfferey von der Nimphen Hercinie*, 107, 137.

[5] See also his apostrophe to a mountain, which, in all probability, is to some extent an expression of genuine feeling: "Du grüner Berg, der du mit zweyen Spitzen Parnasso gleichst, du hoher Felss, bey dir wüntsch' ich in Rhu zu bleiben für und für Und deine Lust gantz einsam zu besitzen. . . . . Natura hat die Lust allher gesetzet, Dass, die auff dich mit Müh gestiegen sind, Hinwiederumb auch würden recht ergetzet" (*An einen Berg*, 26).— Cf. for remarks concerning prospects, Grimmelshausen, *Simplicius*, (XXXIV, 196): "Ich wohnete auf einem hohen Gebürg . . . . von demselben hatte ich ein schönes Aussehen gegen Aufgang in das Oppenauer Thal. . . . ." — Dach, 155: " . . . . Hie wo von Weiten Die Gegend lacht, Wo an der Seiten Der Wiesen Pracht Mich frölich macht. . . . ." — Adam Olearius, *Neue orientalische Reisebeschreibung*, 240: "Wir vertrieben unsere Zeit mit allerhand Lust, wie dann diesen Ort das Wasser, die herumliegende lustige Landschafft . . . . sehr anmuthig machet. . . . ." — It may be noted in passing that this book, though giving an account of a long journey to Persia, contains only few allusions to nature. Cf. Bernhard Richter, Die Entwicklung der Naturschilderung in d. d. geog. Reisebeschreibungen in der ersten Hälfte des 19. Jahrh., Euphorion, Ergänzungsheft V, 6.

Du unerschöpffte Lust, du Wohnhaus aller Freuden, ...
Lass mich, den Ueberfluss der Eitelkeit zu weiden,
Bei deinem Quell' allhier von Sorgen ledig seyn,
Dass dich ja nimmermehr der Sonnen heisser Schein,
Noch deine klare Bach was Trübes thu beleiden.

And *Vom Wolffsbrunnen bey Heydelberg* he writes :

Du edler Brunnen du, mit Rhu und Lust umbgeben
Mit Bergen hier und da als einer Burg umbringt,
Printz aller schönen Quell' . . . .
Vergeblich bist du nicht in dieses grüne Thal
Beschlossen von Gebirg' und Klippen überall :
Die künstliche Natur hat darumb dich umbfangen mit Felsen und Gepüsch.[1]

In the *Schäfferey* we note these characteristic references : "Sie kamen an eine schöne Bach, die mit ihrem silbergläntzenden Wasser die Augen und mit dem lieblichen Geräusche Ohren und Sinnen ergetzete " (118). "Mitten innen nun war das berühmte Quell, dass im Auffschiessen viel kleine Blasen empor warff, an der Farbe aber helle, durchscheinend und auff Art eines weissen Saffirs etwas blaulicht anzuschauen war " (145).[2]

When the poet's interpretation of plant and animal life be considered, there becomes apparent at once his narrow range, as well as his lack of originality. The rose (62, 55),[3] lily (63), sweet marjoram (55, 40), daisy, violet, tulip, and narcissus (40)[4] exhaust the list.[5]   Of trees,[6]

[1] Cf. Horace, *Carm.*, III : 13.— How much more vivid are Spee's lines (82) : " Frisch hin und her gehn zanken Die klare Bächlein krumb Und mit den Steinlein zanken, Wanns müssen fliessen umb."
— Cf. also Dach, 108 : " Lass uns . . . . umb der Bäche Randt . . . . ;" 179 : " Wenn ich in dem Wiesen-schnee ;" 171 : " Wann wir auff begrünter Heyden, Hingestreckt ins feuchte Grass Bey den Bächen, die wie Glass Vor sich rauschen, sollen weiden, Wann die Lerch und Nachtigal An wird stimmen Berg und Thal. . . . ." — Moscherosch (XXXII, 297) : " Es ist zeit . . . . sich bey den frischen quellen In dem grünen zu ergehn. . . . ."

[2] Also 109 : " . . . . nahe bey einem klaren Quelle, das mit anmuthigen Rauschen und Murmeln von einer Klippen herab fiel."—*Trostgedichte*, 276 : " Die Welt lebt in den Tag . . . . ist trotzig aus-gerissen Wie eine wilde Bach." Because of the rather remarkable vivification of the Rhine, the follow-ing lines may find a place here : " Er hat, der schöne Rhein, auss Scham sich fast verloren, Ist weit und breit umher durch kaltes Eiss verfroren " (276).

[3] Cf. Andreas Gryphius (XXIX, 405), *Vanitas ! Vanitatum Vanitas !* where the blooming and the withering of the rose are compared to our own life.

[4] In Logau we note this epigram (196) : " Schmeichler sind wie Sonnenblumen, blicken nach dem Himmel hin, Wurtzeln aber in die Erde suchen Vortheil und Gewinn."— Fleming has these lines (*Auf eines Kindes Ableben*, 17) : " Wo ist der Garten Pracht, der Blumen Königin, der Augen liebe Lust, die Anemone hin, die so nur gestern noch in ihrem Purpur-Munde und keuschem Angesicht' allhier zuge-gen stund ? " — Spee (90) compares grapes glittering on their posts to a well-equipped army leaning on their spears. — Lohenstein (XXXVI, 199) says : " Der Lotus hüllt die Blätter, Die sich früh breiten aus, des Abends traurig ein . . . ."— Cf. furthermore Fleming, *Von den Blumen* (25).

[5] Opitz says of a young lady (*An eine Jungfrau*, 8) : " Wan ihr zu Felde kompt, wohin man euch sieht gehen, Da sieht man alsobald die schönsten Blumen stehen."

[6] See Dach, 182 : " Glück zu, ihr grünen Bäume, Ihr Hauss der Sicherheit, Ihr Vorrath guter Reyme, Schatz aller Fröhligkeit . . . . Ich setze mich hie nieder, und hör euch fleissig zu."

into which is frequently carved the name of, or a sonnet addressed to, his sweetheart,[1] only the pine tree is slightly characterized.[2]

Birds, as might be expected, are oftener mentioned than other animals; and just as the strong eagle, the sweet nightingale, the lark, the ring-dove, the heron, and the owl seek what they like best, so the poet goes in quest of his beloved.[3] He envies the birds their freedom and happiness, for he sings:

> Kompt, last uns aussspatzieren,
> Zu hören durch den Wald,
> Die Vögel musiciren,
> Das Berg und Thal erschallt.
> Wol dem, der frey kan singen,
> Wie ihr, ihr Volck der Lufft . . . .
> Ihr werdet zwar umbgangen,
> Doch helt man euch in Werth,
> Ich bin von der gefangen,
> Die meiner nicht begehrt.[4]

The nightingale, above all, is his favorite bird, if we may judge from the frequency of its occurence in his poems.[5] The bees, that gather honey from violets, roses, and green clover, and are asked to come to the mouth of his beloved,[6] the dove, and the tiger[7] are the only creatures at all particularized. They, like the other animals mentioned by Opitz, are used in similitudes.

His observations about nature in general are interesting, and often serve as a moral lesson. He says that work and rest should alternate, just as there is in nature not always one season, not always rain, nor yet always night (*Schäfferey*, 131). In another place of the same pastoral (116) he declares that nature induces us to travel. Witness the

---

[1] *Pp.* 15, 19, 54, 109, 133, 141.—The linden and the fir tree are often used for this purpose.

[2] Cf. *Vesuvius*, 151. Note also that the elm tree (Gryphius, XXIX, 131) and the cypress (Hoffmannswaldau, XXXVI, 26) occur in similitudes.

[3] *Schäfferey*, 141.

[4] P. 17. Also 139: "Den leichten Vögeln wird ihr Leben gar nicht schwer; Sie fischen in der Lufft gesichert hin und her Und können stets daheim und in dem Ihren reisen."

[5] *Zlatna*, 45; *Lob des Krieges-Gottes*, 87; and *Trostgedichte*, 272. — Especially noteworthy is Grimmelshausen's treatment of the nightingale. The song of the hermit, "Komm, Trost der Nacht, o Nachtigall" (XXXIII, 23), is frequently quoted (cf. Biese, 260; Winter, 23). Winter's statement, "Mit keinem Worte findet sich im weiteren Verlauf der Erzählung angedeutet, dass der wilde Abenteurer . . . . jemals einen Rückfall in diese sentimentale Jugendstimmung bekommen hätte," is not quite true, for Simplicius says (XXXIV, 116): "Einsmals hatte ich mich . . . . unter einem dicken schattigten Baum ins Gras nider gelegt, den Nachtigalen zuzuhören, welcher Gesang mich dann in meiner Betrübnus am allermeisten belustigte, dann ich hörte dieser lieblichen Stimme mit grossem Fleiss zu . . . ."

[6] *An die Bienen*, 26.   *Trostgedichte*, 272; *An Asterien*, 9; *Judith*, 333.

sun, moon, and stars, the flood and ebb of the sea, the fish and the
birds, the poet exclaims.[1]   The order and beauty of nature he admires
in the poem *Vesuvius.*   Here he also mentions the fact that the earth
is never so exhausted as to be unable to reproduce any part of herself.
And finally he asserts that no living thing can exist except through
love.[2]

"Beseelungen" of the parts of nature have already been quoted.
Others should find a place here.   When the poet is sad, not only the
animals, but the very stones, forests, and fields, sympathize with him, in
truly Orphic manner:

Allhier in dieser wüsten Heyd'
Ist gar kein Mensch nicht weit und breit.
Die wilden Thier allein
Die seh' ich selbst Mitleyden tragen,
Die Vögel traurig seyn,
Und mich mit schwacher Stimme klagen,
Die kalten Brunnen starker fliessen,
Viel Threnen gleichfalls zu vergiessen.
Stein, Wälder, Wiesen, Feld und Thal
Hör' ich beklagen meinen Fall.
Sie fühlen meine Pein,
Die Schafe wollen gar nichts weiden,
Du Delia, allein
Wirst nicht beweget durch mein Leiden.[3]

[1] A similar thought in *Trostgedichte*, 289: "Wer hier zu Schiffe geht, Muss folgen der Natur, die
nimmer stille steht."

[2] Cf. *Dafne*, Chor der Hirten, 71.

[3] P. 19.—Cf. *Absterben des Herrn Adams von Bibran*, 40: "Das auch betrübte Grass beklagt
dich bey den Brunnen, ... Es trauert selbst das Rad der grossen Sonnen Und hüllet umb sich her der
Wolcken schwartzes Kleyd; Tranck und Essen Wird vergessen Von aller Herd' und Vieh' ohn Unter-
scheyd . . . . Berg und Thäler hört man ruffen, Bibran, Bibran Tag und Nacht."—Especially when the
poets are unhappy, they appeal to nature, and every part of nature strikes a responsive chord. Thus
Fleming says (*Auf einer abwesenden Jungfrauen Namenstag 4 Sept. 1635*, 43): "Er selbst, der
Himmel steht betrübet, weil er nicht sieht die er so liebet. Mit Regnen weint die blasse Luft. . . . Was
anders können Hirt und Heerden als leid und traurig sich geberden ? . . . . Im Feld, im Pusch', im
Thal', in Auen ist nichts als stille Furcht zu schauen . . . ." Similarly in the poems *An die Stolze*, 67,
and *Als er vergeblich nach ihr wartete*, 103: "Der Himmel treuft mir nach, was ich ihm vor geweint
. . . ."— Spee has these lines (204, 65): "Die Bächlein sollen schwellen auf, Von meinen vielen Zähren."
— Cf. Hoffmanswaldau (XXXVI, 94): "Die Flüsse lieffen an von viel verliebten Thränen, Die
Winde stärckten sich durch seufzerreiches Sehnen."—And Gryphius (*Cardenio und Celinde*, l.
1338): "Der sanffte Westen-Wind . . . . beseuffzet und empfindt Die unaussprechlich Angst, die
meine Seele drücket. Diane, die bestürtzt und dunckel uns anblicket, Bejammert meine Noth . . . ."—
Moscherosch (XXXII, 117) goes into the woods to complain to the birds and to be comforted by their
song.— Heinrich Mühlpfort (XXXVI, 350) sings: "Dunckle Hölen, finstre Schatten, Meines Lebens
Auffenthalt, Wüste Felder, stille Matten, Einsam und verschwiegner Wald, Könnt ihr auch die Seufzer
zehlen, Die ich täglich abgeschickt . . . ."—And Dach exclaims: "Ihr hohen Hügel, heb' ich an, Ihr
Berg', und was sich stürtzen kan, Fallt her mich zu bedecken!" (21).

And when his sweetheart smiles favorably upon him, then he bids them adieu:

> Ihr Birken und ihr hohen Linden,
> Ihr Wüsten und du stiller Waldt,
> Lebt wol mit euren tiefen Gründen
> Und grünen Wiesen mannigfalt.[1]

But also when the poet is in a joyful mood, all of nature sympathizes with him: "..... die grünen Wiesen werden sich freuen umb und umb, es wird Thal, Pusch und Feld ein grünes Kleid anziehn, es werden dir, o Heldt, Die klaren Bäche hier mit Lust entgegen fliessen, Die Felsen höher stehn."[2] Again in *Judith* Abra utters this invocation: "Seyt frölich, Wiesen, Wald und Feld, Erhebt euch ihr Gefilde, Der euch und uns hat nachgestellt, Ist selbst erlegt und umbgebracht. . . . . Lass den Triumphgesang durch Lufft und Wolcken tringen, Es müsse diesen Sieg erheben und besingen Die Erde, Land und Meer" (340, 342).[3]

It goes without saying that Opitz looks upon nature as the work of God. Not a work that He has created and given over to man, but one over which He is always ruling.[4] Comets, rain, thunder, and lightning are His messengers,[5] and all animate nature praises and thanks Him.[6]

---

[1] P. 21.—Cf. also *Echo oder Wiederschall*, 8.—Read in this connection Dach's lines: "Gehabt euch wol, ihr Berg' und Thal, Stein, Brunnen, Pusch und Auen, Wo ich geschertzt so manches Mal, Ich werd' euch nicht mehr schauen" (193).

[2] *Schäfferey*, 130.—In Fleming we note these lines (*Als sie wiederkam*, 117): "Die Luft hat ausgeweint, der Himmel lässt den Flor der schwarzen Wolken ab, der Sturm, der ist vorüber, der West befällt den Wald mit einem sanften Fieber, die hohe Sonne hebt ihr schönes Haupt empor und führet mit sich auf der Blumen ganzen Chor."—In the *Asiatische Banise* (408): "das lager ein solches feldgeschrey erschallen liess, dass bey der stillen nachtlufft die berge durch einen gedoppelten wiederschall ihr mitvergnügen mit grösster anmuth bezeugten."—Similar vivifications are found in Heinrich Mühlpfort (XXXVI, 345): "Die Alabaster Hand lieff ihm auff die Claviren. . . . . Der Wald stund ganz entzückt, die Vögel ganz bethöret, Und schätzten sich beglückt, dass sie den Klang gehöret . . . ." —and Hoffmannswaldau, XXXVI, 70.

[3] For the sake of completeness we add this apostrophe: "Du immergrüner Waldt, Ihr Bäume Jupiters, der Hirschen Aufenthalt, ... Ihr Thäler und ihr Hügel, Ihr Wiesen, Pusch und Feldt, ihr Ort der Einsamkeit, Wer euch besuchen kan . . . . den muss man selig schätzen" (*Vielgut*, 103).

[4] *Klagelied bey dem Creutze unsers Erlösers*, 200. See *Trostgedichtè*, 282: ". . . . der Gott von allen Zeiten, Der auff der hohen Lufft und Wolcken pflegt zu reiten, Der Wasser, See und Meer umbgreifft mit seiner Hand, Die grossen Hügel wiegt, den Himmel überspannt . . . ." Cf. *Vesuvius*, 159.

[5] *Vesuvius*, 161.

[6] *Zlatna*, 55.—Cf. Friedrich Spee (XIII, 111, 112): "Auf auf, Gott will gelobet sein, Du blaues Feld und Wasen . . . . Ihm Lilgen schon und Rosen In gelb und purpur Mäntelein Gar lieb und freundlich kosen."—Adam Olearius (XXVIII, 229) begins his "Neue orientalische Reisebeschreibung" thus: "Dass unser Gott ein grosser Gott ist, erlernen wir unter andern auss dem Buche der Natur, der vernünfftigen Heyden Bibel . . . . So will Gott auch, dass solche Wunderwercke nicht im Verborgen bleiben, sondern von den Menschen betrachtet . . . . werde." But, with the exception of one passage previously quoted, no mention is made of natural scenery (in our edition of his book).

SUMMARY.—The treatment of nature in the works of Opitz and the other writers of the seventeenth century (with but few exceptions, cf. Spee, Dach, and Fleming) is almost altogether conventional. Morning and spring have all the charm for them; night and the other seasons are either not mentioned at all, or a strong dislike for them is expressed. Though winds and thunderstorms are described, yet their majesty does not appeal to the poets of this age. Hills, but not high mountains, are appreciated. Not the grandeur, but the horror and danger of the sea are pictured, and such sea-pictures occur almost exclusively in similitudes. Their favorite landscape is a valley, with a slowly winding brook, a few shady trees, and some distant hills. Their interpretation of plant and animal life shows no originality. It may safely be said that, as a rule, they use nature only to illustrate some human quality or thought, and hence references to nature occur generally in figures of speech. Nature without man they had not yet learned to appreciate.

II.

THE ATTITUDE TOWARD NATURE IN THE EIGHTEENTH CENTURY.

THE artificiality of the seventeenth century hampered free and natural expression. Few dared, or had the ability, to break with the conventionalities of their age, as has been observed in the previous chapter. Before the dawn of a new century, however, was born a poet, a man of feeling, whose verses are rooted in his own experiences. He ushers in "what is most characteristic of the eighteenth century, the growing appreciation of the senses and of the feeling, over against pure intellect." Just about the middle of the century this tendency becomes more pronounced, and grows almost altogether dominant after two or three decades more. To trace the gradual turning of German literature from the artificial to the natural, from indifference to, or ignorance of, the wilder aspects of nature to a closer observation of, and a personal enthusiasm for, nature — such is the purpose of this study.

JOHANN CHRISTIAN GÜNTHER (1695–1723).

In his introduction to Günther's poems,[1] Ludwig Fulda states that the poet uses nature to contrast her with his own mood, or to express his feelings the more fully; he anthropomorphizes her occasionally when he wishes her to take an active part in the vicissitudes and struggles of his own life. It goes without saying, then, that in Günther we are not to look for descriptions pure and simple, such as came in vogue in German literature about Lessing's time, and against which the "Laokoon" was directed. Günther has too much of the true artist's instinct to be satisfied with a mere enumeration of the aspects of nature. In this respect he is far in advance of his own generation, as well as of the succeeding one. He uses nature, that is, as a setting for human emotions. He has the further distinction of being among the first, if indeed he was not the first, to turn from the softer to the sterner aspects of nature; his fondness for night and winter particularly he expresses in no uncertain way.

Allusions to them are scattered throughout his poems. The pale moon is his companion when he is lonely and in sorrow:

[1] Deut. Nat. Lit., 38: 26.

Wie manche schöne Nacht sieht mich der blaşse Mond
In stiller Einsamkeit am Kummerfaden spinnen ! [1]

He inquires of the moon and the stars, of whose influence and power
he feels sure, whether anyone's wretchedness can be as great as his.[2]
He prefers night to day,[3] and expresses his joy at the approach of twilight in the well-known *Abendlied:*

Der Feierabend ist gemacht,
Die Arbeit schläft, der Traum erwacht. . . . .[4]

Of equal significance are his lines on winter:

Der Winter bleibt der Kern vom Jahre,
Im Winter bin ich munter dran. . . . .[5]

It is not, however, its fierceness nor its invigorating effect that endears
this season to him, but rather the defying of its severity by sitting and
smoking at his fire-place.[6]

He turns to nature especially when his love is unrequited. Then
he chooses to avoid man and to associate with the animals of the
forest:

In den Wäldern will ich irren,
Vor den Menschen will ich fliehen,
Mit verwaisten Tauben girren,
Mit verscheuchtem Wilde ziehn.[7]

Günther's life was unhappy throughout, and at times he did not dare
confide his sorrow even to the valleys:

Ihr still-und kahl-und öden Gründe,
Behaltet dieses Wort bei euch:
Ich leid' und darf mich nicht beklagen,
Ich lieb' und fürcht' es euch zu sagen.[8]

The poet calls upon the winds and the waters to convey his greetings
and his sighs to his beloved,[9] or he inquires of them her whereabouts.

[1] *Schreiben an seine Magdalis,* 63.   [2] P. 108.

[3] Goedeke-Tittmann, VI, 125. Cf. also *Lob des Winters,* D. N. L., 38 : 77.

[4] D. N. L., 38:7.   [5] *Lob des Winters,* D. N. L.

[6] *Lob des Knastertobaks,* D. N. L., 38:107.

[7] D. N. L., 38:212. A somewhat similar thought we note in Canitz's *Klageode über den Tod
seiner ersten Gemahlin* (D. N. L., 39: 433): "Ich durchirre Land und Seen; In den Thälern, auf den
Höhen Wünsch' ich wider die Gewalt Meines Schmerzens Aufenthalt."

[8] D. N. L., 38:116.

[9] D. N. L., 38:60, *An seine Magdalis;* 65, *An Leonoren;* 140, *An seine Schöne;* 176, *An Eleo-
noren.*

Unlike the poetry of the First and especially the Second Silesian School, his lines seem to have a genuine ring. He was actually out-of-doors, and not in his study, when he sketched the natural scenery surrounding him :

> Die Gegend, wo ich jetzund dichte,
> Ist einsam, schatticht, kühl und grün;
> Hier hör' ich bei der schlanken Fichte
> Den sanften Wind nach Leipzig ziehn,
> Und geb' ihm allzeit brunstiglich
> Viel tausend heisse Küss' an dich.[1]

When his appeals to his "harte Schöne" prove ineffective, then he concludes that all nature, the gentle breeze, the brook, the birds, and even the ice and snow, have more compassion for him than does she.[2]

Günther's poems appeal to us because they are an expression of a poet's genuine feeling. Now and then he uses a word or phrase current with his predecessors, but on the whole he has broken with their traditions and makes bold to say what he himself feels. He turns to nature in his sorrow, and, unlike Opitz and his followers, shows also appreciation for her sterner aspects. One must conclude, after reading his poems, that without first-hand observation Günther could not have treated nature as he did.

BARTHOLD HEINRICH BROCKES (1680–1747).

The spread of Pietism and the rise of the natural sciences are almost coincident with the turn of the century. Owing to both these influences, the study and observation of nature became more intense than heretofore. The Pietists (Joh. Arnd, Chr. Scriver) as well as the scientists (I. I. Scheuchzer, W. Derham) were of the opinion that the entire study of nature has as its final purpose the knowledge and worship of God. They, however, were not the only ones to entertain this view. After a time they influenced others, chief among them Barthold Heinrich Brockes.[3] As early as 1715 the latter published some descriptive religious poems, which he embodied six years afterward in the first volume of his *Irdisches Vergnügen in Gott.* Eight more volumes were added in the course of the ensuing twenty-seven years, and yet he treated nature as prosaically in his later works as he did in his earlier ones; though in the last three volumes of these he

[1] D. N. L., 38 : 140. Tittmann's ed. (6: 97) has "Schweidnitz" instead of "Leipzig."

[2] Goedeke-Tittmann, 6 : 164, *An seine harte Schöne.*

[3] Brandl, B. H. Brockes, 40 ff.

might well have learned from Thomson, whose "Seasons" he translated. We should, however, not fail to give him credit for the yeoman service he rendered to his own generation : he taught it to observe everything in nature and to observe her moods closely.[1]

Unlike Thomson,[2] Brockes makes ample use of the simile, when he is describing the beauties of nature. These comparisons usually refer to something glittering or gaily colored; metals or precious stones. He rarely fails to see the beauty of each season without thinking of emeralds, or opals, or gold, or silver: " Die Welt ist allezeit schön. Im Frühling prangt die schöne Welt In einem fast smaragdnen Schein. Im Sommer glänzt das reife Feld, Und scheint dem Golde gleich zu sein. Im Herbste sieht man als Opalen Der Bäume bunte Blätter strahlen. Im Winter schmückt ein Schein, wie Diamant Und reines Silber, Fluth und Land."[3]

At other times, however, he is less influenced by his Italian model, the poet Marino, and then gives more poetic expression to his thoughts; for example, in his poems on spring. He says in one of them :

> Alles gläntzet, alles glühet,
> Alles funckelt, alles blühet,
> Durch der Sonnen Gegenwart.[4]

And in another he writes :

> Des beblühmten Frühlings Pracht
> Ist die Sprache der Natur,
> Die sie deutlich durchs Gesicht,
> Allenthalben mit uns spricht.[5]

Intermingled with these rather poetic lines are the following, worthy of a Lohenstein or a Hoffmannswaldau :

> Die schwancken Zweige hängen nieder,
> Und gleichen . . . . dem abwerts hängenden Gefieder
> Von grün beaugten Pfauen-Schwäntzen.[6]
> Das junge Laub scheint sich zu wundern . . . .
> Dass es schon heute durch den West gekitzelt . . . .
> Für Anmuth zittert.[7]

---

[1] Koch, Geschichte der deutschen Litteratur, 142.

[2] Gjerset, Der Einfluss von J. Thomson's Jahreszeiten auf d. d. Literatur, 13.

[3] Irdisches Vergnügen in Gott, II, 107.   [4] Ird. Verg. i. Gott, V, 35.

[5] Ibid., I, 38. Cf. also IV, 27, 37, 38; V, 5, 26, et passim. A favorite epithet of spring is " lau," IV, 107, 116, etc.

[6] Ird. Verg. i. G., V, 11.   [7] Ibid., IX, 321.

And yet, side by side with such bombast and unnaturalness are to be found first-hand observation and, to some extent, genuine feeling, as his several poems on autumn show. The poet sees the intermixture of green, yellow, and red leaves, and the harmony thereof,[1] and rejoices at the coming of this season: " Willkommen, kühler, traubenreicher, mit süssem Obst beladner Herbst, Der du die Wälder übergüldest, mit rothem Glanz die Früchte färbst, Die Welt in bunten Flor verhüllst . . . ."[2] No less delighted is he in the approach of winter—a season heretofore disliked and dreaded.[3] He notes the glittering of ice and snow in the sunlight: "Wie funckelt nicht das Eis! Wie schimmern, gläntzen, blitzen, Die durch der Sonnen heitern Strahl So wunderschön beflammten Spitzen Von Zacken, Reif und Schnee?"[4] He watches with intent interest the falling snowflakes,[5] and as he looks out upon the snow-covered fields he remarks:

> Nicht ohne Regung unsrer Brust
> Erblickt man weisse Felder.
> Die Wipfel der beschneiten Wälder
> Erregen uns besondre Lust.[6]

When walking, he hears the crackling of the snow at every step.[7] The frost on the window panes attracts his attention.[8] Skating he mentions as one of the pleasures of winter.[9] But at heart he prefers to stay in his warm home, where he can drink wine and eat baked apples.[10] He is certain that in due time spring will supplant the winter, and therefore says consolingly: "verzweifle nicht, wenn rauhe Winde wehn "[11]—a thought that calls to mind Geibel's poem "Und dräut der Winter noch so sehr."

Brockes's power of observation ever asserts itself. It can be seen in his comments on the effect of sunlight or moonlight as it falls upon the hills, the trees, or the water. In the morning he sees the red mountain peaks and the reddish-yellow treetops,[12] and later in the day he observes the light shining through the interlacing leaves: " Es sind die Blätter dicht, Und doch so dünn und zart, Dass selbst das Licht Durch ihr so angenehm gefärbt Gewebe bricht, Sich mit den röhtlichen gelinden Farben par't."[13] The dancing shadows of the

---

[1] Ibid., II, 434. [4] Ird. Verg. i. G., I, 481. [7] IV, 394.

[2] IX, 391. [5] Ibid., IV, 431; VI, 198. [8] I, 335; IV, 427.

[3] Cf., however, Günther, p. 16. [6] Ibid., V, 376. [9] I, 324.

[10] III, 625. His *Betrachtung einer sonderbar schönen Winter-Landschaft* (IV, 415) should not be overlooked.

[11] IV, 419. [12] I, 183; VIII, 136. [13] I, 82; II, 28, et passim.

trees and the ever-changing light they cast on the ground, or on the water, are noticed by him.[1] After a rainfall the whole forest seems to him glittering and sparkling;[2] and when the day is cloudy, then he enjoys the dim light: " Es färben sich die Wolcken falb' und grau : Doch mischt sich ein klares Blau In diese Dunckelheit, Dadurch vergnügt so dann ein dämmricht Licht Und trübe Klarheit das Gesicht."[3] Moonlight, however, pleases him still more : it calls forth some of his best lines. Thus he describes a quiet moonlight night when nothing is heard but the song of the nightingale: " Es war die holde Nacht . . . . Die Luft war lau und still . . . . Der Silber- farbne Schein Des eben vollen Monds erfüllt mit sanftem Strahl Wald, Wiesen, Gärten, Berg und Thal. Ein' ungemein' und angenehme Stille Regieret' überall."[4] Of even greater interest is the admiration he manifests for a field of snow with the moon shining full upon it,[5] since it was many years before such a scene appealed to the æsthetic sense of poets.

Brockes's sensitiveness to colors and odors is rather remarkable. He distinguishes between the green of the linden, the willow, the box- tree, the cypress, and the myrtle.[6] In spring he sees " auf allen Zweigen Ein liebliches Gemisch von braun und grün sich zeigen . . . . gelblich-grün [der zarten Blätter] und dunckel-grün [der Büsche] sich mischen."[7] He mentions seven colors of the anemone,[8] and observes with like accuracy the shining white, black, and red coats of horses and cows grazing at sunset.[9] He is especially fond of the word " falb," and applies it to rivers, shadows, clouds, etc.[10] He is more observant than his predecessors or contemporaries in recording the odor of fresh-mown hay, of lilac, and of camomile.[11]

His treatment of plant and animal life is marked by breadth rather than depth. His range of observation is wide, but he lacks the ability to interpret poetically. After examining a flower microscopically, so to speak, he puts into rhyme the result of his observations. Compare his lines on the sunflower and the chestnut blossom.[12] He mentions the crown-imperial, the hyacinth and haw, and calls the primula veris " holdselig Frühlings-Kind."[13] Only the comment on the " Merz- Veilchen " has something of the modern touch :

[1] I, 202; II, 30, 182, etc.
[2] I, 202; VIII, 38.
[3] V, 42.
[4] IV, 84; V, 185, et passim.
[13] IV, 15; VI, 28; I, 258; IV, 30.

[5] IV, 425.
[6] II, 120.
[7] V, 29.
[8] V, 67.

[9] IV, 316.
[10] I, 150, 193; II, 42, etc.
[11] I, 188; VI, 133.
[12] II, 406; III, 595.

> Willkommen, liebstes Frühlingskind,
> Du Bild der Demuth und der Liebe ! [1]

The dense forest is his favorite place of refuge "vom städtischen beschwerlichen Getümmel." [2] He does not characterize trees in any near sense, but applies to all of them the epithet "kraus." [3] Of animals he knows a goodly number — his long lists are well known — yet he fails to make any but prosaic remarks about them.

We have already noticed that Brockes has a word to say of almost everything in nature. He walks along the seashore and sees "die Brandungen der Wellen aus ihren Tiefen sich erhöhen, sich bäumen, wallen, brausen, schwellen, mit einem knirschenden Geräusch . . . . das Ufer zu verschlingen drohn." [4] The wave, the waterfall, or the brook is to him an image of life.[5] His poems contain one or two mentions of hills,[6] but have much more to say of cornfields. Thus he exclaims on one occasion: "Wie angenehm bewegt sich hier das blonde reifende Getraide !" [7] Of especial interest, however, is the fact that Brockes calls attention to the heath, the grandeur of which finds no poetic expression until many years later. Our poet says of it : "Betrachtet man sie recht so . . . . sieht man wunderbar in ihr der Farben Pracht, der Bildung Zier fast unverbesserlich verbunden." [8]

But what is his purpose in observing and studying nature ? may be finally asked. It is not for her own sake, but rather to learn thereby more of the greatness and goodness of God. The poet leaves small room for doubt that this is his chief purpose when he expresses this outspoken opinion: "Bringt die Betrachtung [eines Baumes] dich sodann nicht auf die Spur Von der durch Gottes Macht stets wirkenden Natur . . . . So sag ich ungescheut, Dass du ein Atheist, Ein Vieh, ein Klotz, ein Fels, ja noch was gröbers bist." [9] Like so many of his contemporaries, he was influenced by the Bible and shared the view of nature held therein. He believes that all creatures sound the praises of God, the birds as well as the flowers.[10] God created everything for some use or purpose, and Brockes makes it his purpose to discover these utilitarian qualities, which to his mind demonstrate the wisdom of the Creator. In this attempt, however, he is prone to grow, not only prosy, but — what is worse — ridiculous. Such passages as the following have tended to bring him into disrepute :

---

[1] II, 15.   [2] I, 200; IV, 339, etc.   [3] I, 57, 94, etc.

[4] VII, 109. Cf. *Die Fläche des Meeres im Sturm* (VII, 87) ; *Die Schönheit eines stillen Meeres* (VII, 91).

[5] II, 140, 114, et passim.   [7] IX, 366.   [9] I, 73.

[6] I, 104; II, 36.   [8] *Die Heide*, II, 224.   [10] V, 126.

Nebst dem Balg ist auch am Fuchs seine Lunge, Fett und Blut
Gegen Schwindsucht, Krampfbeschwerden, Blas' und Nierenschmerzen gut.
Wird man also abermal auch in Füchsen offenbar
Einer Ordnung, Weisheit, Absicht, wenn man es erwägt, gewahr![1]

Instead of quoting the stock illustration about the chamois, it were perhaps well to cite the passage which sets forth the usefulness of every part of an ox:

Aus den Hörnern macht man Kämme, Pulverflaschen, Messerheften,
Löffel, Dosen, Schreibzeug, Büchslein, zu so mancherley Geschäfften . . .
Aus den Knorpeln und den Nerven wird der zähe Leim gemacht . . . .
Aus dem Unschlitt macht man Lichter und auch Seifen . . . .
Nichts ist besser als das Mark für geschwächte Nerv und Sehnen.[2]

As both these passages occur in the last volume of the "Irdisches Vergnügen in Gott," we are led to believe that Thomson's influence upon him could have been, at best, only slight.

Brockes rendered a service to German literature that may, in some respects, be compared to Thomson's work in the English field. He was dissatisfied with the conventionalities and narrow limits of poetry, and attempted as best he could to enlarge the horizon. He lacked, however, the necessary genius to carry out successfully so stupendous a task. Hence he sank into oblivion, when greater men appeared on the scene of action, and even the credit to which he is justly entitled was withheld from him. He had taught his generation to observe nature, not as treated by the poets, but as found round about them. Everything that he beheld in the external world called forth some comment from him, and though in this way he opened the eyes of many to the hitherto unobserved beauties of nature, yet at the same time he made his lack of poetic fire even the more obvious.

ALBRECHT VON HALLER (1708–77).

"Haller," says Scherer,[3] "kommt in unserer Litteratur dicht nach Günther." But only in his youth does he evidence points of resemblance to the senior poet. His earlier poems are rather passionate and, like Günther's, written in the language of Lohenstein. His later ones, however, show a marked change, as will be seen presently. To his poem *Die Alpen* he owes his importance in the history of the nature-sense, not so much in that he thereby awakened the romantic feeling for these mountains — this was left to Rousseau — but that he helped to increase and disseminate the new interest in Switzerland.[4]

[1] IX, 256.   [2] IX, 260.   [3] Litgesch., 372.
[4] Friedländer, Ueber die Entstehung und Entwicklung des Gefühls für das Romantische in der Natur, 16.

Just as was the case in his travels through Germany, Holland, and England (see p. 91), Haller pays more attention to the people than to Swiss scenery,[1] though he goes to Switzerland with the full intention of seeing " la nature, et non pas . . . . les hommes, ni leurs ouvrages."[2] At times he points out, like Brockes, the usefulness of nature's products; at other times her moral influence upon the Alpine dwellers is uppermost to his sense.[3] The passages in which he depicts nature for nature's sake are few in number. The description of the St. Gotthard is one of them :

> Ein angenehm Gemisch von Bergen, Fels und Seen
> Fällt nach und nach erbleicht doch deutlich ins Gesicht;
> Die blaue Ferne schliesst ein Kranz begländter Höhen,
> Worauf ein schwarzer Wald die letzten Strahlen bricht.
> Bald zeigt ein nah' Gebirg die sanft erhobnen Hügel,
> Wovon ein laut Geblök im Thale widerhallt;
> Bald scheint ein breiter See, ein meilenlanger Spiegel,
> Auf dessen glatter Fluth ein zitternd Feuer wallt;
> Bald aber öffnet sich ein Strich von grünen Thälern,
> Die hin und her gekrümmt, sich im Entfernen schmälern.[4]

The lines about the gentian, well known from Lessing's "Laokoon," constitute another of these passages :

> Dort ragt das hohe Haupt am edlen Enziane
> Weit übern niedern Chor der Pöbel-Kräuter hin;
> Ein ganzes Blumen-Volk dient unter seiner Fahne,
> Sein blauer Bruder selbst bückt sich und ehret ihn.[5]

Besides "Die Alpen," Haller's minor poems should be taken into account. In the earlier ones he uses certain of the conventional phrases of his predecessors: he speaks, for example, of moss as the carpet of nature, or compares the color of sky and clouds to sapphires and rubies.[6] Such expressions are not found in his later poems. Here we have rather genuine feeling and vivid description. Read some of the lines *An Herrn D. Gessner* (1733):

[1] Cf. also Oliver Goldsmith, The Traveller.   [2] See letter, July 16, 1728.   [3] Winter, Programm, 26.

[4] About forty years after the publication of *Die Alpen*, Bonstetten says of it: " Warum hat Haller in seinen Alpen nicht die schaudernden Scenen des Gotthards oder Grimsels besungen ? Seine Manier ist nicht die von Salvator Rosa, der die erhabne Unordnung der Natur so schön malte." (Letter to Müller, Lugano, Nov. 25, 1773.)

[5] To Lessing's criticism on these lines Haller replies in the *Tagebuch*, I, 277: " Der Dichter will blos einige merkwürdige Eigenschaften des Krautes bekannt machen, und dieses kann er besser als der Mahler: denn er kann die Eigenschaften ausdrücken, die inwendig liegen, die durch die übrigen Sinne erkannt, oder durch Versuche entdeckt werden, und dieses ist dem Mahler verboten (z. B. die Regenfarben des Thaues, etc.)."

[6] *Sehnsucht nach dem Vaterlande,* 1726; *Morgen-Gedanken,* 1725.

> Sieh, wie die trunknen Auen blühn!
> Die Wälder deckt ein schönes Grün . . . .
> Die dürrsten Anger werden bunt,
> Ein jeder Busch hat seinen Mund . . . .
> Bald lockt dich Flora nach der Au
> Wo tausend Blumen stehn im Thau,
> Die auf dein Auge buhlend warten.

Just as really does he show the change in attitude, the turning to nature, when at the death of his beloved Mariane he would fain seek the densest forest, devoid of light, and the dead fields and terrible valleys, where brooks empty into desert swamps. "Dass ich," says the poet, "doch bei euch des Todes Farben fünde! O nährt mit kaltem Schaur und schwarzem Gram mein Leid! Seid mir ein Bild der Ewigkeit!"[1]

As has been observed, *Die Alpen* is Haller's chief work from the standpoint of our study. If one consider the possibilities in the treatment of such a theme and what Haller made of it, he can scarce be ranked high among the poets of nature. Contrary to his own statement, his chief concern is with man, and not with nature. As a scientist he had to observe her, and hence his descriptions are based on his own observations. Though he helped, no doubt, to increase interest in the Alps, yet he did not leave to us a just appreciation of these mountains. Not before Goethe's "Schweizer Briefe" can German literature boast of such a work.

FRIEDRICH VON HAGEDORN (1708–54).

Haller and Hagedorn are often put in juxtaposition.[2] It was Haller himself who pointed out the similarities and differences in their lives, characters, and works. He informs us that both wrote verses at an early age, and in their youth were fortunate enough to visit England, to become acquainted with English literature, and to be influenced by it.[3] But the differences between them are more apparent. Haller traces them back to the following circumstance: Hagedorn was of a light disposition; he drank wine, and enjoyed the pleasures of friendship. He himself, however, ceased drinking wine in his nineteenth year, because he was troubled with continuous

---

[1] *Trauer-Ode beim Absterben seiner geliebten Marianne*, 1736, and *Unvollkommenes Gedicht über die Ewigkeit*, 1736.

[2] Cf., for example, Scherer, Gesch. d. d. Lit., 372.

[3] Cf. Hagedorn's letter to Gottlieb Fuchs (Sept. 15, 1752): " Folgen Sie [in der Schreibart] immer den Engländern, oder vielmehr der Natur."

headache. Hence he withdrew from jolly company and sought pleasure in reading. Thus arose the great difference in the style of their poetry: Hagedorn wrote light, lyrical verses in the manner of Horace and Anacreon; Haller composed serious didactic poems, modeled upon Virgil. Their views of nature differed accordingly: Hagedorn was pleased with the gentler aspects of nature; Haller turned to the more majestic. At the beginning of their career their interpretation of nature was more or less conventional; later on they were rather given to write from actual observation.

It follows from Hagedorn's view of nature that in his poems day and spring receive fuller treatment than do night and the other seasons. In his descriptions of the former he evinces considerable appreciation and genuineness of feeling. Compare, for example, "Der Morgen," which begins thus: "Uns lockt die Morgenröte In Busch und Wald." The poet speaks of the joy of the birds, mentions the fertile fields, the glittering "Schmelz" of the green plains, the chase of the doe, and then tells us how at the break of day the herdsman and his love are thrilled with joy. A few times he uses the sunrise in similitudes.[1] The night he bids welcome, because it is hostile to care and worry, but chiefly because it offers better opportunity than day for the indulgence of sensual pleasures.[2]

In spring, nature and man are full of pleasing.[3] The charming songs of the nightingale and of the soaring lark, the clattering of the wandering storks and the prating of the tricky starling, the merry shepherd and his herd, the sprouting of the leaves and flowers, the rippling brooks—all these come with the advent of spring.[4] Then the poet gives vent to his feelings in the well-known lines:

> Du Schmelz der bunten Wiesen!
> Du neubegrünte Flur!
> Sei stets von mir gepriesen!
> Du Stille voller Freuden!
> Du Reizung süsser Lust![5]

Of the phenomena of the sky Hagedorn describes at length only the wind and the thunderstorm. A fairly detailed, but by no means adequate, picture of a storm is drawn in *Der Zeisig*—a poem for which he found no model in any other author, and which, therefore, contains in all probability a record of some of his own observations. It begins thus: "Der Mittag kommt umwölkt. Die grauen Mewen

[1] I, 14, 69.   [2] *Die Nacht.*   [3] *Horaz*, l. 7.   [4] *Der Mai.*
[5] *Empfindung des Frühlings.* Cf. also *Der Frühling*, III, 99.

fliegen Mit bangem Flug, und schreyn, und nähern sich dem Lande;
Allein und unglücksvoll spazirt im trocknen Sande Die dunkle
Kräh, und scharrt; Gewitter, die verziehn, Ruft sie mit Krächzen
her. Tief um das Schilfgras streichen Die Erdschwalb' und der
Spatz . . . . Mit aufgerecktem Hals schnauft der beklommne Stier.
Die Pferde treiben sich die Stalle zu erreichen. Schnell überwältigt
ein Wirbelwind den West, Der Hain erbebt und heult; auf Ficht
und Tanne schossen Verwüstend der Ocean, der Regen und die
Schlossen . . . ." A similar description, but not as extensive, is found
in *Der Wein*, where a great shout of joy is compared to the roaring
of the winds in the tops of the trees. Now and then the poet alludes
to the furious raging of Eurus and Boreas,[1] but only once does he
mention how lovingly, how gently, the western winds warm the shore,
the hill, the cave![2] Of clouds, their shape and color; of the ocean,
when calm or stormy — of these phenomena which, in later years, were
to arrest the attention of poets, Hagedorn has nothing to say.

In his interpretation of inland scenery, the brook receives most
mention. When he compares the fame of an author to a brook which
flows on, turbid and lazy, through gravel and mire, which bends and
creeps, and, increased by other waters, rushes on proudly to finally
bear the name of river;[3] or when he likens a noble heart to a clear
brook, which winds along through meadows, neither rushes nor hurries,
yet fructifies its banks, where grow the flowers with which the shepherds garland themselves in spring[4] — then we see that Hagedorn
uses in similes that feature of the rural landscape which later the
Anacreontic poets employed extensively. Hills are barely mentioned,
and the wood and the cool grove are treated rather conventionally.[5]

When we turn to his interpretation of the plant and animal world,
we note at once the very narrow range of the one and the wide range
of the other. This difference may, perhaps, be due in part to the
fact that Hagedorn translated and composed many fables, and thus
gained a more intimate knowledge of animals. He merely mentions
by name such flowers as rosemary, sweet marjoram, wild thyme,[6] and
once compares a young man to the garden clover shooting upward
in time, and unlike the sluggish aloe that produces late blossoms.[7]

---

[1] *Der Weise; Der Affe und der Delphin.*   [2] *Der Mai*, ll. 25 ff.   [3] I, 81.   [4] I, 170.

[5] I, 13. Of his charming retreat, Harvstehude, he sings (III, 143): "Hier gehet in gewölbten
Lüften Die Sonne recht gefällig auf, Und lachet den beblümten Triften, Und sieht mit Lust der Alster
Lauf." Cf. letters, May 16, 1751, and June 23, 1745.

[6] *Der Falke*, l. 239.   [7] III, 137.

The almost total absence of roses in his poetry[1] is indicative of the fact that he is not Anacreontic through and through. His use of trees is limited even more than that of flowers.[2] With fishes and birds, on the other hand, he is much better acquainted. He considers him happy who angles in the pond or stream, where tench and carp leap, and trout and loach are crowding.[3] He listens to the song of birds, the nightingale, the lark, "[denn] ihr buhlerischer Lustgesang verehrt und lobet lebenslang die freye Liebe."[4] He is glad of the cuckoo's call, because it announces the return of spring, and "so lange seine Stimm' erschallt, wird weder Gras noch Laub erbleichen."[5] He speaks of, or merely mentions, such birds as siskin, magpie, linnet, woodpecker.[6] To other animals he refers occasionally, sometimes using them in similes.[7]

In common with many of his contemporaries, Hagedorn preferred country life to city life, because it was free from care and worry. He sings its praises repeatedly, most fully in *Horaz* and in *Die Landluft*. Here we read :

> Geschäfte, Zwang und Grillen,
> Entweiht nicht diese Trift ;
> Ich finde hier im Stillen
> Des Unmuths Gegengift . . . .
> Es webet, wallt und spielet
> Das Laub um jeden Strauch . . . .
> Und alles, alles lebet,
> Und alles scheint verjüngt.
> Die Reizung freier Felder
> Beschämt der Gärten Pracht,
> Und in die offnen Wälder
> Wird ohne Zwang gelacht.

The life of the peasant and of the shepherd is to his mind preferable to that of the courtier and the townsman, because it is simpler and plainer.[8] It approaches somewhat the life of the Arcadian age—a state of happiness still extant among the gypsies, upon whom Hagedorn showers endless praise.[9] This turning to the original state in nature, and away from civilization with all its conventionalism and corruption, points unmistakably toward the movement of which Rousseau became, not many years later, the most ardent exponent.

Hagedorn looks upon nature as the work of God, as a manifestation

---

1 Only two references were noted, *Der Traum*, l. 25, and I, 22.

2 Laurel, birch, oak, pine, and lime tree are merely mentioned.

3 *Horaz*, l. 149.   4 *Die Vögel.*   5 *Der Guckguck.*   6 II, 62.

7 *An Celsius.*

8 I, 32.

9 *Lob der Zigeuner.*

of His power and strength.[1]   All nature listens to His words and all beings sound His praises.[2]

Hagedorn's view of nature may be characterized as idyllic, and, as he himself tells us, was largely influenced by Horace and the pastoral writers.   Therefore we need not expect any appreciation of the grand and majestic in nature, but only of her gentler aspects.   He goes to his country seat' whenever he can, to be away from the turmoil of the city.   There he composes his spring songs,[3] which, because of their felicitous expressions, have endured to this very day.

THE ANACREONTICS.

Though English influence is more or less evident in Brockes, Haller, and Hagedorn, it is more apparent still in some of their immediate followers, as is clearly shown by their strong aversion to rhyme.   They, therefore, turned to a poet whose verses were light and easy and without rhyme.   They took Anacreon's poetry for their model, not because of its content, but because of its form.[4]   It was formerly supposed that they had become familiar with Anacreon through Hagedorn;[5] now it is generally accepted that Anacreontic poetry in Germany took rise in the University of Halle, in or about 1738, and that its first promulgators were Gleim, Uz, Götz, and Rudnik.   They did not adhere to this kind of poetry all their lives, but, owing to their influence, other men (Wieland, J. G. Jacobi, Klamer Schmidt) culti- vated it, even as late as the seventh and eighth decade of the century.

JOHANN LUDWIG GLEIM (1719–1803).

Gleim, the most voluminous writer of the group, uses nature in a way typical of the Anacreontic school.   This is truer of his earlier poems than of his later ones, for in the former the joyful aspect of nature, in the latter the religious view, is more predominant.   Though he follows rather closely in the footsteps of his predecessors, yet here and there a bit of first-hand observation is recognizable.

In the morning he invites us to see the sun rise : " das Licht der Welt, Wie's kommt und in die Thäler fällt, Und auf der Berge Spit- zen."[6]   He reproaches those who sleep when Aurora reddens the roofs,[7] for they fail to appreciate the first indications of the power and magnificence of the sun, which is but an expression of God's will and might.[8]   All praise the golden beams of the sun, says the poet,[9] man

---

[1] I, 8.   [4] Hettner, Litgesch., III, ii, 94.   [7] V, 338.

[2] I, 7.   [5] See his works, III, 209, for an appreciative estimate of Anacreon.   [8] I, 323.

[3] IV, 159.   [6] I, 372.   [9] I, 47.

and brook and dale, mount and crag and mead. As he sits at the door at sunset, he is filled with emotion and exclaims:

> Welche Kühle, welche Wonne,
> Welch ein schönes Abendroth!
> Wie so sanft stirbt dort die Sonne,
> Seht nun ist sie todt![1]

Then he describes the scene at twilight:

> Mücken tanzen im Getümmel
> Unter sich im Abendgrau;
> Über uns ist heller Himmel;
> O wie dunkel ist sein Blau!
> O wie leise, wie gelinde
> Wehn die kühlsten Abendwinde!
> Welchen hohen Flötenschall
> Singet Meister Nachtigall
> Um sich her in stille Lüfte,
> Blumen duften süsse Düfte.[2]

The stars, and especially the moon, which he calls once "Gedankenfreund,"[3] make night beautiful for him.[4] Several times he expresses the conventional idea of the moon extinguishing by its greater brightness the light of the stars,[5] but uses only once or twice the classical name Luna instead of "Mond."[6]

His comments on spring are more plentiful, but show just the same lack of poetic interpretation. It is, of course, a time of gladness and joy; the birds and flowers appear, the air is mild again, the tyrannic rule of winter has come to an end.[7]

> Schwalb' und Storch und Kibitz sind gekommen,
> Seinen Zephyr hat der Lenz genommen;
> Veilchen hauchen in erwärmte Lüfte
> Balsamsüsse Düfte.
> Junges Grün ist schon hervorgesprossen,
> Schollen sind den Bach hinabgeschossen. . . . .[8]

In the month of May, especially, all creatures — the bees, nightingales, larks, lambs — are full of life and joy.[9] Gleim invites his friend Fischer

---

[1] VII, 100.   [2] VII, 30.

[3] VII, 155. This probably shows Klopstock's influence. Note also *An den Mond* (VII, 272):
" Als ich noch dein Scheinen sah, Du mich noch fandst am Pulte, da war eine Nacht noch schön."

[4] I, 40, 170; VII, 47.   [6] II, 19; I, 40.   [8] *Einladung*, I, 308.

[5] V, 130; I, 40.   [7] *Des Landmanns Frühlingslied*, I, 367.   [9] II, 117.

to come out into nature and watch the pervading and pulsating life everywhere:

> Im Stillen und im Todten regt sich Leben überall!
> Im kleinen Tannenwalde schlägt die erste Nachtigall,
> Die Lerche singt in hoher Luft,
> Die Biene summt, der Kuckuck ruft!
> Welch ein allmächtiges Gewühl im Reiche der Natur,
> O welche Kräfte, welch Gefühl
> Im Busch und auf der Flur![1]

Autumn and winter are treated in accordance with tradition. They are disliked because they rob us of foliage, shade, and flowers, and drive the birds from their green cells into the shadows or cliffs.[2]

Leaving aside a few conventional uses of the ocean,[3] we turn for a moment to such phenomena of the sky as the winds, thunder, and lightning. Most references are, of course, to gentle zephyrs playing with the locks of lovely girls.[4] Lightning is used in comparisons[5] and together with thunder is considered the most direct expression of God's power. After a thunderstorm we shall see, says Gleim,[6] "den Schöpfer der Natur in seinen Werken, Auf uns'rer Blumenflur, In uns'rem Weitzenbau, Ihr Kinder umgeschaut! Die ganze Feldflur steht Wie eine schöne Braut!"

In investigating Gleim's interpretation of inland scenery, two features that show the influence of idyllic poetry may be noted — the purling brook and the shady tree. There the lovers rest and listen to the babbling spring.[7] Gleim, like the other Anacreontic poets, wishes his life to flow on peacefully like a brook.[8] He uses the brook in similes,[9] or personifies it, as the following lines show:

> Wie murmelt er so lieblich, wie fliesset er so hell!
> Er reizt, er überredet, wie Chloens Mund zum Kuss.[10]

When he is sad the brook sympathizes with him: "Mitleidig, lieber Bach, ist dein Getön, du tröstest, seufzest, stimmst in meine lange Klage; lieber Bach, du schwillst von meinen Thränen!"[11] This is an illustration of the sentimentality characteristic of the elegiac idyllic poetry before Goethe. Brooks, hills, herds, and a wood, endless wheat-fields, and all surrounded by bushes — these constitute a beautiful landscape, according to Geim.[12]

---

[1] II, 127.   [3] IV, 96; VI, 67.   [5] II, 202; VI, 24.   [7] II, 70.   [9] II, 320; VII, 255.

[2] I, 80.   [4] III, 19; V, 108.   [6] VII, 43.   [8] II, 91.   [10] II, 131.

[11] *An den Panka-Bach*, VI, 142.   Cf. Friedrich Spee, p. 12, note 3.   [12] *Die Landschaft*, VII, 106.

His treatment of plants and animals shows hardly any first-hand observation. He mentions them by the score, but fails to individualize them. Of the rose, which occurs more than sixty times, this is perhaps the most interesting comment: " dich zu sehn, und vertraut mit dir zu sprechen, welche Wollust!"[1] The lines on the violet have a more genuine ring :

> So lieb, so klein, so schön, so rein,
> Lieb Veilchen auf der Heide!
> Lieb Veilchen, du die kleinste Zier
> Der Mutter Erde, du bist mir,
> Bist mir die grösste Freude![2]

The forget-me-not, pink, sunflower, jasmine, clover, lavender, lilac, are merely mentioned by name.[3] This is true also of Gleim's trees. Besides the myrtle, laurel, and oak, the fir, beech, linden, maple, and yew tree are found.[4] Of birds, too, he knows a considerable number. The nightingale is a messenger of love and, like the lark, the harbinger of spring.[5] The poet is sorry that the swallow cannot speak, for, if she could, he would inquire of her about the streams and brooks, where a dear friend dwells.[6] The quail, swan, peacock, eagle, hummingbird, are also referred to.[7] He does not seem to be well acquainted with fishes,[8] but shows familiarity with domestic and forestine animals. Sheep and lambs he represents as joyous or sad, corresponding with the shepherd's every mood.[9] The influence of pastoral poetry is obvious here. When Gleim speaks of animals, he often grows prosaic, reminding one of Brockes. Compare these lines: "Auf den Blüthen uns'rer Linden Sammeln Bienen Wachs und Honig ; Auf den segensvollen Fluren Sucht der Hamster seinen Weitzen, Und die Ameis' in dem Garten Sammelt Nahrung für den Winter."[10]

Like so many of his generation, Gleim expresses the utmost hatred and contempt for city life. He can hardly have based his observations on his own experience, for the little town of Halberstadt, where he resided, could scarcely have exhibited the hurry and bustle, nor its inhabitants the flattery and treachery, of which he speaks in *Lob des Landlebens:* "Gottlob, dass ich dem Weltgetümmel entflohn, und unter freiem Himmel Nun wieder ganz mein eigen bin! Entfernt

---

[1] II, 126.
[2] *Das Veilchen*, II, 195.
[3] II, 83; I, 50, 157, 323; III, 52.
[4] I, 154, 255; II, 149, et passim.
[5] I, 266.
[6] *An die Schwalbe*, VII, 141.
[7] V, 82, 174; VII, 95, 98, et passim.
[8] II, 223 (trout); V, 146 (herring); VI, 312 (oyster).
[9] I, 146; V, 73.
[10] I, 69.

vom Schmeichler und Verräter . . . ."[1] To shun the arrogance of townsfolk he concludes to become a shepherd, and invites his friends to go with him to the forest and fields.[2] The peasant, too, desires to keep aloof from the morbidity of the city, for he says: "Was sollt' ich in der Stadt Die kein gesundes Pferd In ihren Mauern hat?"[3] He sees no reason for envying kings or courtiers; his own state seems to him to be the happiest. He sings:

> Wie selig ist, wer ohne Sorgen
> Sein väterliches Erbe pflügt!
> Die Sonne lächelt jeden Morgen
> Den Rasen an auf dem er liegt.[4]

The reapers and sowers, the plowmen and gardeners, too, sing songs in which they find expression for their happiness and content.[5] This feeling, which permeates the eighteenth century, that those are the happiest who are away from civilization, finds its fullest and most felicitous expression in the works of Rousseau.

In Gleim's later poetry, as has been already stated, the religious view predominates. He believes God to be in everything — in the sun, moon, and stars; in the thunder, lightning, and tempest; in the tree, grass, and flower;[6] but guards against the accusation of Spinozism by saying: "Ich meine, dass die Welt von Gott verschieden ist."[7] He is convinced that God created everything in nature for a purpose, and that all is subject to His will.[8] All nature shows His omnipotence and praises His goodness.[9] As in Brockes and Haller, so in Gleim we note the influence of the Bible (cf. Psalm 104). As he acknowledgedly did not possess much poetic fire (like Brockes), he may be suspected of trying to make up in quantity what he lacked in quality. Composing his poems after the manner of Horace, Anacreon, and the pastoral, he failed to add anything new to a better appreciation of nature. His interpretation coincides largely with Hagedorn's, except in point of sincerity: Gleim's verses often show on the surface lack of actual experience.

JOHANN PETER UZ (1720–96).

Uz has more of the true poet in him than Gleim, and evinces therefore deeper and more genuine emotion in his treatment of nature, though it must be conceded at the outset that his range of observation is not much wider. Like his fellow-poet, he describes at length

---

[1] I, 197.   [2] I, 173.   [3] I, 388.   [4] Der glückliche Landmann, I, 374.
[5] Lied der Schnitterinnen, des Säemanns, des Pflügers, des Gärtners, I, 349–66.
[6] VI, 62, 176, et passim.   [7] V, 372.   [8] V, 69.   [9] VI, 18, 45.

morning and spring. He intersperses now and then conventional
phrases in his poems, as the following lines show :

> O seht, wie über grüne Hügel
> Der Tag, bekränzt mit Rosen, naht !
> Ihn kühlen Zephyrs linde Flügel :
> Vom Thau glänzt sein beblühmter Pfad.
> Wie taumelt Flora durch die Triften !
> Die Lerche steigt aus trunkner Saat,
> Und singt in unbewölbten Lüften.[1]

Evening is agreeable to him, for it is then that he hears the amor-
ous complaint of the nightingale resounding on the quiet air,[2] but the
night he dislikes : " Die schwarze Nacht verbreitet wieder ihr melan-
cholisches Gefieder."[3] He makes almost no mention of the moon.[4]

He notes the change in the appearance of the earth with each new
season, and, of course, in winter also. He says rather interestingly:
" Und nun ihr müder Leib in weissem Schmucke glänzt."[5] In spring
he is naturally most effusive. These lines in the famous poem *Der
Frühling* are typical :

> Es lacht die ganze smaragdene Flur . . . .
> Und auch die ganze Natur fühlt sich aufs Neue begeistert,
> Da sich die Sonne der Erde genaht ;
> Und jedes frostige Thal, so Wald als grüne Gebirge
> Sind reg und alle Gefilde belebt.[6]

The thought that in spring the young man's fancy gently turns to
thoughts of love is reiterated in several poems, for example, in *Früh-
lingslust:* " Seht den holden Frühling blühn !—Fühlt ihr keine Früh-
lingstriebe ? . . . . In der frohen Blumenzeit Herrsche Bacchus und
die Liebe ! "[7] While he gives vent to his joy in this season of the
year, he does not forget that the equinoctial storms are invariable con-
comitants of early spring.[8] Autumn and winter are, on the other
hand, dreary seasons, for then the trees are leafless and the rough
winds blow in the deserted garden.[9] Yet—and here we see his Anacreontic trend of mind—for love and wine it's not too cold.[10]

To the phenomena of the sky and atmosphere there are few allusions. Twice he speaks of red lightning, and once he uses a rain

[1] I, 48.

[2] *Der Abend.*

[3] I, 229.

[4] The only references are I, 194, and II, 101.

[5] II, 27.

[6] Cf. also *Empfindungen an einem Frühlingsmorgen.*

[7] Cf. I, 115, 135.

[8] *Sehnsucht nach dem Frühling.*

[9] II, 253.

[10] *Der Winter*, I, 128.

cloud in a simile.[1] Though he mentions rough winds now and then, yet it is the gentle zephyr, sighing and soughing in the foliage, that he uses most profusely.[2] Sea-pictures occur in a few similitudes, and here as elsewhere the sea is thought of as wild, stormy, and roaring.[3]

Uz's inland scenery is like Gleim's : " Felder, durch die ein lautrer Bach mit heischerm Murmeln schleicht," [4] sums up practically his conception of landscape. He attributes also human qualities to the brook, when he says, " lispelnd nährt ein Bach die Schwermuth seiner Seele," or when he compares the passing of the days in the arms of the beloved to the gentle flow of the brook, " der unter finstern Sträuchen, Von hohen Bäumen rund umwacht, Stets ungerunzelt lacht." [5] Like Gleim, he, too, compares his life, not to a mountain torrent, as some later poets have done, but to a brook flowing quietly among the bushes.[6]

In his interpretation of plant and animal life Uz is not more original than is Gleim, and his range of observation, too, is much narrower. The rose and the lily are the subject of his song. The sight of the former stirs his blood and makes him wish to see "ein blühend Mädchen," while of the latter he says : " die Lilie buhlt umsonst nach seinen starren Blicken." [7] Even the white blossoms that fall on Laura's grave seem to be in love : " Hier herrscht die Liebe! scheinen sie zu sagen. Hier herrscht die Liebe! seufz ich nach." [8] In his treatment of trees classical influence is most apparent. The myrtle and laurel are spoken of repeatedly, whereas other trees receive scarcely more than bare mention.[9] Very little can be said of Uz's observations in the animal world. Hardly any individualization is attempted.[10] Only these lines on the raven may be quoted : " Der junge Rabe, der beschneyet Hoch auf nackten Wipfeln schreyet, sättigt sich aus deiner Hand" (*Lob des Höchsten*, I, 284), and the curious comparison of an earthquake to a horned owl : " Die Erde hat gebebt . . . . Wie aus bemoostem Schutt der Uhu, wann die Nacht In furchtbarn Schatten ihn verstecket, Auf stille Dächer fliegt, selbst melancholisch wacht, Und heulend müde Städte wecket" (*Das Erdbeben*).

City life is distasteful to him because of the "Weltgetümmel," as Gleim says elsewhere, and hence the wise man goes to the country, where he finds needful rest : " O Wald! o Schatten grüner Gänge!

---

[1] I, 92, 260; II, 250. Gleim also speaks of red lightning, VI, 24.   [5] II, 30, 255.   [6] I, 78; II, 16.
[2] I, 96; II, 161, et passim.   [3] I, 246; II, 58.   [4] I, 81.   [7] I, 117; II, 31.   [8] I, 242.
[9] I, 276 (cypress), 301 (oak), 115 (beech), 152 (elm), 72 (linden) ; II, 30 (pine), 308 (poplar).
[10] I, 67 (nightingale), 166 (lark) ; II, 217 (swallow).

Geliebte Flur voll Frühlingspracht! . . . . Ich fühle mich wie neugeboren, Und fang erst nun zu leben an."[1] The same idea Uz emphasizes in a letter to the privy councillor B.:[2] "Nur auf dem Lande kennet, fühlet und geniesst man die Natur." Therefore he praises the life of a shepherd and, what is more, of uncivilized man.[3] Nature is beautiful at all times, and these are her charms: "Die fette Flur geziert mit angenehmen Grün, Die Berge, niedern Thäler; Fröhliches Gewühl auf herdenvollen Matten, Gebüsche voll Gesangs, und stiller Wälder Schatten, Hier See, dort felsicht Land, und aus dem dunkeln Hayn die Quellen murmelnd fliehn."[4] To lie on the grass and rest from work and worry in the midst of such scenery is indeed a treat.[5]

Uz, like the other Anacreontic poets, shows the influence of the Bible, when he says that God keeps unceasing watch over this wonderful world, and manifests His presence in the ocean, in the worm, in the gently swaying grass, and in the fierce storm.[6] We trust in Him and praise Him who gives to the earth sunshine, rain, and dew, "dass frisches Grün um ihre Glieder, Ihr Haupt mit jungen Blumen lacht, Und ihren mütterlichen Rücken Saat und milder Segen drücken."[7] The poet emphasizes the absolute order and law in nature, and says of her in a way anticipatory of nineteenth-century thoughts on evolution: "Natur, die niemals flüchtig springt, und stufenweise nur auf ihrer güldnen Leiter steiget."[8]

Uz, even more than Hagedorn or Gleim, is distinctively a poet of spring. His joy in this season is felicitously expressed in various poems, especially in *Der Frühling*. His range of observation is not wider than that of his contemporaries, but his descriptions are more poetical.[9]

JOHANN NIKOLAS GÖTZ (1721–81).

The dislike of city life and the fondness for country life which are so clearly expressed in Gleim and Uz, are equally emphasized in the poems of the third associate, Johann Nikolas Götz. He invites his friend Crollius to come to the country, that he may escape the smoke of the city, and the noise of drums, and the sound of trumpets.[10] "Städte sind der Aufenthalt des Stolzes, Und der Sorgen und der Leidenschaften," he exclaims.[11] But valleys, gardens, and brooks are

---

[1] *Der Weise auf dem Lande.*   [3] *An die Freiheit.*   [5] I, 19.   [7] *Lob des Höchsten.*
[2] II, 218.   [4] II, 27.   [6] II, 43.   [8] I, 188.

[9] In how far Uz was influenced by Anacreon and Horace, Erich Petzet has shown in Zeitschrift f. vergl. Litgesch., VI, 328–92.

[10] Pt. I, 53.   [11] Pt. II, 164.

the places where one can dream in poet's fashion. He greets the country in these words : " Du Sitz der Ruh, Holde · liebenswerthe Wüste. . . . ."[1] With the exception of a few " Beseelungen," which we shall note presently, his poems add nothing new to the treatment of nature as found in Gleim and Uz. Of the poppies he says at dawn of day: " des Mohnes Blumen, Die die Köpfchen melancholisch hängten, Ihren nahen Sterbetag betrauern ;"[2] and of violets : " Gross von Geist, wiewohl von Leibe klein, An Glanz und Farbe schön, doch sittsam und gemein.[3]

KLAMER EBERHARD SCHMIDT (1746–1824).

Klamer Schmidt, whose fame rested in the eighth decade of the century on his imitations of Petrarch and Catullus, is generally con-sidered one of the late Anacreontic poets. He is more modern than they, having learned, no doubt, from the men who wrote in the sixth and seventh decades. Owing probably to Young's influence, the melancholy features of nature appeal to him. Unlike the Anacreon-tics, he is fond of describing evening and night. They are character-ized in *Triumph ihres Blickes* (1776) better than in *Petrarka's Selbstgespräch* (1771) or in *Abendgesang*, and therefore the lines may be quoted here :

> In sternbesä'tem blauen Mantel lag
> Am Himmel schon die lieblichste der Nächte,
> So schmachtend schön, als ob sie noch den Tag
> Durch ihren Reiz zu übersiegen dächte!

His melancholy trend of mind finds its best expression in the *Kirch-hofselegie* (written before 1778), where this passage is found :

> Herrlich, herrlich ist des Sommers Neige,
> Wenn der Nord auf öden Gräbern hallt,
> Wenn vom Wipfel düstrer Ulmenzweige
> Blatt auf Blatt, sich kreisend niederwallt . . . .
> Horch ich ahne.— Ruf der Todesgötter,
> Stark und immer stärker hör' ich dich,
> In dem Seufzen hingefall'ner Blätter!
> Holder Ruf, wann foderst du auch mich ?

JOHANN GEORG JACOBI (1740–1814).

Another of the late Anacreontic poets, but better known than Klamer Schmidt, is Johann Georg Jacobi. His most significant poems appeared from 1775 to 1782,[4] and do not come, therefore,

---

[1] *Die Einsamkeit auf dem Lande.*   [3] Pt. II, 88.
[2] Pt. III, 178.   [4] Cf. Works (Zürich, 1809), III, Preface, 3.

within the scope of this treatise. We refer to such poems as *Morgen-lied*, *Sommertag*, *In der Mitternacht*, *Die Linde auf dem Kirchhofe*, all of which evince a deeper feeling for nature and express this feeling in more poetic language than do his early productions. These latter, however, concern us here. In them, as in the other poems of this class, a strong love for the country and for spring, and an equally marked dislike of winter, are noticeable. Thus he writes from the country about the natural scenery surrounding Halle: "Hier redet die Natur Im fernen Wald, auf naher Flur, In ungekünstelten Alleen, An meinem Hügel hier, im Klee . . . ."[1] He is sorry for the woodsman that merely counts the trees, and measures them, and fails to appreciate the charms of spring that delight the poet. "Liebe Nachtigall! Schöner Blüthenregen! Wie die Knospen all, Unter Lerchenschlägen, An der Quelle sich bewegen! O wie lieblich alles ist!"[2] In winter, on the other hand, he sees nothing but dreariness and desolation, and hears "der Dohlen heiseres Geschrey, und Winde die sich müde schwärmen," and beholds everywhere "der Schwermuth Bild, in finstre Wolken eingehüllt."[3]

CHRISTOPH MARTIN WIELAND (1733–1813).

Although usually not classed with the Anacreontic poets, Wieland has much in common with them, so far, at least, as the choice and treatment of many of his themes are concerned. He differs from them, in that he is a far better master of poetic form and expression than they. Like the poems of the Anacreontics, however, his literary productions, especially his early ones, do not contain, as a rule, a record of his own experiences. This is certainly true of his treatment of nature. We find no traces in his works of the beautiful scenery of southern Germany, or the majestic highlands of Switzerland; and yet he lived and traveled in both countries for many years (see Letters, p. 78). Strange to say, it is the same Wieland who says, in speaking of the readers of Milton: "Wer beim Anblick einer wild-anmuthi-gen Landschaft ungerührt bleiben kann; wer die Sonne untergehen sehen kann, ohne eine angenehme Aufwallung in seinem Herzen zu fühlen: der wird kalt beim Milton bleiben."[4] Yet he himself seems to be unmoved, or at least does not give expression to his feelings, when he beholds the grand or terrible in nature. Only the gentler aspects, spring and moonlight scenes, are treated of. When he sees

[1] *An meinen Bruder.* [2] *Der Hirt und der Förster.* [3] *Winterreise,* 6.
[4] *Abhandlung von den Schönheiten des epischen Gedichts "Der Noah"* (1753).

the snow dissolving, and hears the nightingale and lark,[1] then he goes outdoors: "wo mich mit einsamen Schatten Blühende Hecken umwölben, will ich, o Frühling, Dich fühlen mit eröffnetem Herzen."[2] Of all his characters Araspes and Agathon show the most feeling for nature. The one enjoys the gentle moonlight, the charming contrast of the faint colors, and the quiet of the night, as opposed to the bright hues and the loud turmoil of the day ;[3] and the other is infatuated "von den Annehmlichkeiten des Mondscheins, von der majestätischen Pracht des sternenvollen Himmels, von der Begeisterung, welche die Seele in diesem feierlichen Schweigen der ganzen Natur erfahre."[4] Araspes in his sorrow turns to nature to find a wild and lonely spot away from man. "In Wildnisse will ich fliehen," he exclaims,[5] ". . . . wo die Natur nie lächelte, wo alles todt um mich her ist, verlassen und einsam." And again: "Stille Natur! Ich will Deinen Athem, die frische blumige Luft einziehen und in Deinem mitleidigen Schatten meine Thränen mit der weinenden Quelle vermischen."[6] But he, too, who is seeking true joy wanders to the quiet brook, to the very heart of nature, to shun the tumult of the city.[7]

Like the Anacreontics, Wieland sees love and God manifested everywhere in nature, as he tells us in *Araspes und Panthea* and in *Natur der Dinge* (Bk. I). Order and law in nature are due to His power. "Die weise Macht . . . . wehrt dass die Natur nicht Epikurisch hüpft!"[8]

That Wieland had some feeling for nature cannot be gainsaid. It was faint, to be sure, but it did not lack genuineness. He was more interested in describing what he saw and felt than in noting what others had failed to observe. Otherwise he could not have spent so many years in Switzerland without leaving in his works a record of his impressions. He no doubt assisted to bring into vogue what was later designated "Mondscheinpoesie."

CHRISTIAN EWALD VON KLEIST (1715–59).

With Brockes's translation of Thomson's Seasons (1744) descriptive poetry gained a strong foothold in Germany, and most men of letters

---

[1] *Natur der Dinge*, Bk. IV.   [2] *Lobgesang auf die Liebe.* Cf. *Der Frühling.*

[3] *Araspes und Panthea*, Pt. II, 2. Cf. also *Idris*, Canto IV, st. 29, and *Don Sylvio*, Bk. V, ch. 12, especially Bk. II, ch. 6.

[4] *Agathon*, Bk. II, ch. 5. See also ch. 4, and Bk. VI, ch. 2; Bk. IV, ch. 1.

[5] *Araspes und Panthea*, Pt. II.   [7] *Musarion*, Bk. I.

[6] Cf. also *Der neue Amadis*, Canto I, st. 19.   [8] *Natur der Dinge*, Bk. I.

were soon to be influenced by it. The earlier poems of Wieland are of this kind; they show more than a mere passing familiarity with "The Seasons" and with Ewald v. Kleist's *Frühling* (1749)—the first poem in German literature after the manner of Thomson. "The Seasons" and *Der Frühling* were now read and imitated by many poets whose names have been almost forgotten. In regard to Kleist it should be remembered that he had not always written in the Thomsonian spirit; in the poems that appeared before *Der Frühling* we can find distinct traces of Brockes's influence.[1] In these poems we note also that longing for rest and peace in nature, and the desire to be away from man. He says in *Sehnsucht nach der Ruhe*:

> O Silberbach, der vormals mich vergnügt,
> Wann wirst du mir ein sanftes Schlaflied rauschen?
> Glückselig! wer an deinen Ufern liegt,
> Wo voller Reiz der Büsche Sänger lauschen. . . . .

Only then can one be happy, as he tells us in the famous line: "Ein wahrer Mensch muss fern von Menschen sein!" Like the Anacreontics, he, too, was influenced by Horace in his eulogy on country life, which he addresses to Ramler:

> O Freund, wie selig ist der Mann zu preisen,
> Dem kein Getümmel . . . . den Schlaf entführet. . . . .
> Er sieht auf Rosen Thau, wie Demant blitzen; . . . .
> Er geht in Wälder, wo an Schilf und Sträuchen
> Im krummen Ufer Silberbache schleichen.[2]

Biblical influence also is discernible in some of his minor poems. Compare *Lob der Gottheit* and especially his *Hymne*, which calls to mind some of Friedrich Spee's lines: "In finstern Wäldern will ich mich allein Mit dir beschäftigen. Und seufzen laut und nach dem Himmel sehn, Der durch die Zweige blickt; Und irren an des Meers Gestad', und dich In jeder Woge sehn. . . . ."

Unlike Brockes, Kleist could and did undergo a marked change in his view of nature after reading Thomson. His evident love of nature, so poetically expressed in the *Frühling*, is descanted upon in his prose writings. He says in one of his essays: "Das grosse Reich der Natur . . . . bietet uns tausend erlaubte Ergötzlichkeiten dar. . . . . Der Felder und Auen beblümte bunten Decken prangen für uns . . . . alles füllt unser Gemüth mit Freude und Entzückung."[3] This joy in nature he sets forth in the *Frühling*.

---

[1] Gjerset, Der Einfluss von Thomson's Jahreszeiten, etc., 20.

[2] *Das Landleben.*   [3] II, 227. Cf. *Irin*, II, 39.

> Empfangt mich, heilige Schatten! Ihr Wohnungen süsser Entzückung,
> Ihr hohen Gewölbe voll Laub und dunkler schlafender Lüste. . . . .

and

> Es lachen die Gründe voll Blumen, und alles freut sich, als flösse
> Der Himmel selber zur Erden!

are typical passages. Some of the vivifications in this poem, as, for example, the following, are well worth noting:[1]

> Aus Wollust küssen die jungen Blüthen einander und hauchen
> Mit süssem Athem sich an.

Thomson's influence is obvious in this description of the coming of spring:

> Auf rosenfarbenem Gewölk, bekränzt mit Tulpen und Lilien,
> Sank jüngst der Frühling vom Himmel. . . . .

As he looks through the bushes, a vista opens before him:

> Voll laufender Wolken der Himmel, und ferne Gefilde
> Voll Seen, und buschige Thäler, umringt mit blauen Gebirgen.

The lines

> . . . . ein sanftes Tönen erwachte
> Und floh und wirbelt' umher im Hain voll grünlicher Dämmerung

are certainly modern in spirit. Over the poem as a whole there rests a fresh and healthy atmosphere, and, as we also know from his letters, the poet's knowledge of nature is to a large extent first-hand. In spite of his smallness of range and feebleness of observation, he is the first, and perhaps the only, one that can justly be named with Thomson.

FRIEDRICH WILHELM ZACHARIÄ (1726–77).

It was Kleist himself who styled Friedrich Wilhelm Zachariä "ein wahrer deutscher Thomson."[2] To the student of today, who knows Zachariä by his mock heroics alone, this appellation may seem entirely erroneous. Although it must be borne in mind that in his own time Zachariä was well known as a descriptive poet, yet it may be truly said without prejudice that Kleist's estimate of him is misleading. Zachariä's *Tageszeiten* are an unsuccessful imitation of "The Seasons." Many of his descriptions are not based upon actual observation, and are therefore often grossly exaggerated.[3] Of interest, however, is the delight he takes in the melancholy features of nature, showing as it does a

---

[1] Cf. Hagedorn's and Bodmer's letters (Sept. 24, 1751, and Jan. 27, 1751 (?)) for an appreciation and a criticism of *Der Frühling*.

[2] Letter to Gleim, Oct. 21, 1755.   [3] Gjerset, Einfluss von Thomson's Jahreszeiten, etc., 43–5.

considerable acquaintance with Young's "Night Thoughts." The poet sits down amid the ruins of an abbey at twilight, when the dismal moon casts her flickering light on the terrible and lonely cloisters, and no sound is heard except the complaining notes of the owl, or the rustling leaves of the ivy.[1] Another melancholy spot is pictured thus : "ein krummes, verwachsenes Thal, ... rund umher mit rauhen steilen Felsen umgeben, von denen nur einige wilde Gesträuche traurig und malerisch herabhängen."[2] To such a place the deceived lover turns : "ihm sind die hangenden Felsen, Und das grausende Thal, ein sympathetischer Anblick, Denn ein Eden würde noch mehr in Schwermuth ihn stürzen."[3]

The Hartz mountains, which were almost totally ignored in literature until Stolberg's time, attract Zachariä's attention, because of their wild, terrible, and melancholy aspect. There he wishes to saunter in the evening : "Last uns dort das rauhere Thal, o Muse, besuchen, Und am hangenden Felsen, in langen schrecklichen Wäldern kühn einhergehen."[4] He believes that these mountains are almost devoid of loveliness, for he addresses the Hartz thus : "So lass auch den heutigen Tag mit aller der Anmuth dich schmücken, Die einen Harztag zu schmücken vermag."[5] He fails to understand how his friend can live in the Hartz mountains in winter, when the valleys are covered with snow and the storm howls in the fir trees ; so he invites him to come to the town.[6] In summer, on the other hand, the poet takes refuge in the country, to be away "from the noise and tumult of the wide city."[7]

Love for the melancholy features of nature, such as we have just seen in Zachariä's works, is not found in the poetry as studied thus far. Now the time has come when Young is to influence certain of the German writers, among them Zachariä. This one, in his anxiety to look for terrible and melancholy spots, fails to observe the charms of the Hartz mountains, which Stolberg discovered not much later.

SALOMON GESSNER (1730–88).

Idyllic and pastoral poetry was produced in Germany, as has been seen, in the seventeenth and eighteenth centuries. The source of inspiration for the Anacreontics, as well as for many other poets, is to be sought in the bucolics of classical (Virgil, Horace) and modern

[1] *Die Vergnügungen der Melancholey*, Bk. V, 144. Cf. Gray's Elegy in a Country Churchyard.
[2] *Lagosiade*, Bk. I, 345.   [4] *Der Abend*, Bk. IV, 116.   [6] Bk. III, 101.
[3] *Der Abend*, Bk. IV, 113.   [5] *An den Harz*, Bk. III, 91.   [7] Bk. III, 136.

(Pope) writers. No one in Germany, however, expressed the spirit of this kind of poetry better or more fully than did Salomon Gessner. In his "Idylls" (1756) pastoral poetry found its true culmination. They were well suited to a generation that had turned away from real life, to seek comfort and consolation in an ideal, in a primitive world, and hence they were not only widely read in the original, but also in the other languages, into which they were soon translated. They are of little interest to us today, except for the illustrations which Gessner himself supplied. These prove conclusively that he knew more of art than of poetry, for there is occasionally a depth and tenderness of poetic feeling in his engravings not to be found in his "Idylls."[1] He draws from nature, as he tells us in a letter to Fuesslin concerning landscape painting, and also after the works of the masters, and then learns by comparison. He is acquainted with Thomson and Brockes (who in his time was rapidly sinking into oblivion), and advises painters to learn from them. But what of the nature-sense in his "Idylls" and other works?

In them, as in his letters, he shows some appreciation only of the gentler aspects of nature, whereas the majestic Alps, in the midst of which he dwelt nearly his whole lifetime, are nowhere mentioned, not even by name. It cannot be said of him, as it has been said of Kleist, "dass er seit langer Zeit wieder der Erste ist, bei welchem Leben und Dichten untrennbar zusammengehen."[2] Since he was writing for a generation that was morbidly longing for Arcadian times, he could and did introduce only those features of nature that were compatible with peaceful and happy pastoral life. Hence spring and moonlight are always a part of the background of the canvas, on which he portrays, not genuine rustic life, but the life of shepherds, as he found it described in the French court-poetry. His Daphnis looks up to the quiet moon and sighs: "So lieblich ist sie, so schön wie du Mond! So schön gegen den andern Mädchen, wie du gegen den andern Lichtern, die um dich her schimmern."[3] Mehala sits in the pale light of the moon, "selbst blass wie der Mond in Wolken gehüllt."[4] As night draws on, and peace reigns supreme, the poet grows ecstatic and exclaims: "O! wie schön ist alles in der sanfteren Schönheit! Wie still schlummert die Gegend um mich! Welch Entzücken! . . . ."[5]

Like so many other writers of his generation, he detested city life and went to nature to find true rest and happiness.[6] One of his

1 Oeuvres traduits de l'Allemand—A Zuric, chez l'auteur, 1777.   2 Hettner, Litgesch., IV, 103.

3 Daphnis, Pt. II, 19.   4 Der Tod Abels, Pt. I, 248.   5 Die Nacht, Pt. II, 153.   6 An den Leser.

characters, Arates, expresses this thought : " Die Eindrücke, die diese Anmuths-volle Gegend auf mich macht, sind so lieblich, dass es scheint, meine Seele empfind es, dass der Aufenthalt bey der einfältigen schönen Natur unserm Wesen der angemessenste und zuträglichste sey." [1] It is nature undefiled by human hand that he prefers. "Ach Natur! Natur!" exclaims Aristus,[2] " wie schön bist du ! wie schön in unschuldiger Schönheit, so dich die Kunst unzufriedner Menschen nicht verunstaltet !" When Aeschines lauds the formal garden of the French, then Menalkas points out the more beautiful natural grove with its winding walks.[3]

Of the four seasons, winter with its storms is, of course, the most disagreeable; the others are pleasing to him.[4] In his comments on autumn we note probably the first genuine appreciation of this season. It is again Menalkas who says of it : " Was für ein sanftes Entzücken fliesst aus dir itzt mir zu, herbstliche Gegend ! Wie schmückt sich das sterbende Jahr ! Gelb stehn die Sarbachen und die Weyden um die Teiche her. . . . . Ein röthlichtes Gemische zieht von dem Berg sich ins Thal, von immer grünen Tannen und Fichten geflekt. Schon rauschet gesunkenes Laub unter des wandelnden Füssen . . . . nur steht die röthliche Zeitlose da, der einsame Bote des Winters." [5]

Gessner was read more widely than perhaps any other eighteenth-century writer, not only in Germany, but, through the medium of translations, in France and England as well. He owed his popularity to the theme he had chosen : the portrayal of idyllic life was well suited to a generation that was longing for a simpler mode of life. He clearly expresses the desire for nature undefiled by human hand, and, as a matter of course, prefers the natural park (of Kent) to the formal garden (of Le Nôtre). In his appreciation of autumn he stands alone among his literary associates.

FRIEDRICH GOTTLIEB KLOPSTOCK (1724–1803).

About the year 1740 there flourished in Halle two groups of poets : a younger group, the Anacreontics, and a slightly older group, represented by Pyra and Lange. These were of a more serious turn of mind ; they had been influenced by pietistic doctrines and followed more or less closely Haller and Milton.[6] Though they, together with the Swiss critics, Bodmer and Breitinger, made the very favorable reception of Klopstock possible, they could hardly have had any

[1] *Der veste Vorsaz*, Pt. III, 123, 150. [3] Pt. III, 82. [5] Pt. III, 94.

[2] Pt. II, 76. [4] *Lycas*, Pt. III, 61. [6] Scherer, Litgesch., 419.

influence upon him in his view of nature, for they remained indifferent
toward nature or treated her in a conventional way. In his *Noachide*,
Bodmer (1698–1783) draws upon nature for a few similitudes,[1] which
show as little actual observation as do the following lines :

> Den duftenden Hauch, des Odems Erstlinge fassten
> Junge Zephyr' auf güldene Flügel, und eilten die Beute,
> In die bräutliche Kammer zu tragen ; die Nachtigall tönte
> Festlich das Brautlied ; . . . . das ganze Gebirge
> Ward musikalisch, die Symphonie sass den wehenden Westen
> Auf die Schultern, und mischte sich unter den Weihrauch der Blüthe.[2]

Of much greater importance, and, in fact, most significant, are some of
his comments in his critical works. In distinguishing the difference
of effect that the beautiful and the grand produce upon him, he
declares that when he looks upon a small farm-house, in the midst of
fields and woods and alongside a clear brook, he feels a sort of pleasure which makes him wish to live all his life in such a charming place.
When, on the other hand, we behold, he says, certain limitless objects,
such as wide stretches of land or large deserts, terrible masses of
mountains or high cliffs and precipices, or, again, a wide expanse of
water, we become agreeably frightened and, as it were, are cast adrift,
to experience a delightful tranquillity of soul. " Da würcket nicht die
Schönheit auf das Gesicht, sondern die wilde Pracht, welche in diesen
erstaunlichen Wercken der Natur hervorleuchtet."[3] Not many years
after Bodmer had written these lines, there arose a poet in Germany
who felt and expressed " diese wilde Pracht der Natur."

In reading, from our point of view, the works of Klopstock and
James Thomson, we come upon a curious parallel : their earlier
works, the Odes and the Seasons, show genuine love of nature ; their
later ones, the dramas, contain but few scattered and rather unimpor-
tant references to nature ; while their letters of this later period still
bear witness to a love of nature as real, if not as active, as that of their
youth.[4]

Of Klopstock's dramas, *Der Tod Adams* (1757) and *Hermanns
Tod* (1784) are the most valuable for our present purpose. As Adam
bids farewell to this world, he addresses the beautiful fields, the mountains, the shady valleys, where he was wont to walk and breathe life
and joy, "wo ich so oft glückselig gewesen bin . . . . von euch nehm

---

[1] Canto IV, XII.   [3] *Critische Betrachtungen über Gemälde der Dichter*, 211.

[2] P. 122.   Reynolds, Treatment of Nature, etc., 86.

ich heut feierlich Abschied!"[1] In *Hermanns Tod* is found the sentimental fisher's song, of which the winding brook is the theme : " Er
hatte kleine Strudel, Wie Grübchen im Kinn. Sein Rauschen war
Gelispel, Er murmelte; Es waren keine Worte, Und ich verstand ihn
doch . . . . Er kam aus der Kluft hervor, Dort hatt' er lang sich
gekrümmt und gewunden, Hatte Wehmuth gerauscht."[2] In the other
dramas nature is drawn upon occasionally for conventional similitudes,
as in *David* (1772), where warriors are compared to lions; or in *Hermann und die Fürsten* (1787), where Hermann's fighting is likened to
the rushing of a mountain stream; or, lastly, in *Hermanns Schlacht*
(1769), where the battlecry sounds " wie das Weltmeer an dem Felsen-
gestade."[3]

More references to nature are found in the *Messias* than in Klopstock's dramas, and they are generally in the form of similes. He
employs chiefly the phenomena of the sky (such as dawn, dusk, moon),
or water (brook, torrent, ocean), or storms, but hardly ever succeeds in
drawing a clear and distinct picture.

Joseph walked in the assembly, quiet as the peaceful moon in the
cloud high above us, and Eve led the youth " [da] silberfarben wallte
der Mond, der Stern, sein Gefährt, stand, funkelt' am weisslichen
Himmel."[4] The following lines are characteristic of the use of nature
in the *Messias:*

> Wie ein Stern, und noch einer, und wieder einer hervorgeht
> Aus der gränzlosen Tiefe der schauererfüllenden Schöpfung,
> Wenn der kommenden Nacht die Abenddämmerung weichet :
> Also versammelten sich die erscheinenden Gottes auf Tabor.[5]

Of the moon it is said that " enthüllt vom Gewölke . . . . schimmerte
[er] sanfte Gedanken herunter denen, die noch im Schlafe nicht
lagen "[6] — a thought which recalls to mind the opening lines of *Die
frühen Gräber*, written at about the same time. The dawn, which
occurs in a few similes,[7] is spoken of at length in Canto XIX (l. 268):

> Und den Strahl des werdenden Tages milderte lichter
> Nebel ein Schleyer aus Glanz, und weissem Dufte gewebet.
> Ruh war auf die Gefild' umher, sanftathmende Stille
> Ausgegossen. Ein Nachen entglitt da langsam-sichtbar
> Voll von Freuden dem lieblichen Duft des werdenden Tages.

Water, in one form or another, is used only in similes. The music

---

[1] Zweite Handlung, Erster Auftritt.   [2] Scene 17.   [3] The moon is mentioned in scenes 3, 8, 10, 11.
[4] Canto IV, l. 21 ; XVII, 305, 418.   [5] Canto XV, ll. 1371 ff.   [6] XV, 482 ff.   [7] III, 476, 497, et passim.

of the harp is compared to the murmuring of a distant weeping brook, the noise of the lamenting multitude that surrounds the cross of the Savior is likened to the sound of mountain torrents, and the reverberations of the song resound like the "Hain, wenn weit in der Ferne Ströme durch Felsen stürzen; und nah von den Bächen es rieselt : Wenn es vom Winde rauscht in den tausendblättrigen Ulmen."[1] The crowds of people rush on like the billows of the ocean, and "Gedanken (drängten) andre Gedanken, Wie Wogen des Meers, wie der Ocean drängte, Als er von drey Welten dich, fernes Amerika, losriss."[2]

In other similes rage, or fierce passions, are compared to tempests.[3] Thus we read in Canto XIV: "Sie vermochten nicht mehr zu widerstehen. So reisst sich Durch den Wald der stärkere Sturm. Die Bäume des Waldes Zittern, rauschen mit Ungestüm alle, beugen sich alle, Vor dem herrschenden Sturm, der Donnerwolken, und Fluten Himmelstürzender Meere von Berge treibet zu Berge!" The following picture also shows the haziness characteristic of the *Messias* as a whole: "Aber wie zwey Gewitter, die an zwo Alpen herunter Dunkel kommen (ein stärkerer Sturm tönt ihnen entgegen, Wird sie verstreuen!) wie die in ihrem Schoosse den Donner Fliegend reizen, damit er die krummen Thäler durchbrülle, Also rüsten sich wider Eloa die stolzen zur Antwort."[4] An awful uproar of all the elements in nature will announce the day of resurrection :

> Rauschen werden die Ströme! die Stürme brausen, das Weltmeer
> Brüllen! beben die Erde! der Himmel donnern, und Nacht seyn![5]

Less vague than these lines are the few passages in which vivifications occur. The cedar, the wind, the torrent, the ocean, are asked to speak of God, or to be at rest when He makes His presence manifest.[6] When Abadonna repents, he seeks the Savior at the sources of all rivers and exclaims : "In aller dämmernden Haine Einsamkeit hat sich mein Fuss mit leisem Beben verloren! .... Ich sprach zu dem hangenden Berge: Neige dich, einsamer Berg, nach meinen Thränen herunter."[7]

The hazy atmosphere which hovers about the *Messias* and makes the reading of the poem tedious to the modern reader, because of the lack of clear and distinct pictures, is by far less perceptible in the *Odes.* They are based on Klopstock's experiences, and were written for the most part before he became altogether "seraphic" and oblivious of

---

[1] XX, 495 ff.   [3] IV, 276, et passim.   [5] XI, 608.

[2] II, 835.   [4] VIII, 139.   [6] I, 360; V, 186, 492.   [7] Canto V.

the world of nature round about him. We agree with Winter, when he says of Klopstock's nature-sense : " In den Dichtungen Klopstocks finden sich die durch Wärme der Empfindung und liebevolle Hinge-bung verklärten Bilder der wirklichen Natur . . . . am häufigsten in den früheren Oden." [1] He has in mind *Der Zürchersee* (1750), " Schön ist, Mutter Natur, deiner Erfindung Pracht . . . . ," *Die frühen Gräber* (1764), " Willkommen, o silberner Mond, Schöner, stiller Gefährt der Nacht . . . .," and *Die Sommernacht* (1766), " Wenn der Schimmer von dem Monde nun herab In die Wälder sich ergiesst . . . . ." To these we may add *Friedensburg* (1751), in which this bit of fine description occurs : " Sieh den ruhenden See, wie sein Gestade sich Dicht vom Walde bedeckt, sanfter erhoben hat, Und den schimmernden Abend In der grünlichen Dämmerung birgt . . . . ," *Die Frülingsfeyer* (1759), with its powerful description of an approaching thunderstorm, and *Der Eislauf* (1764) — a poem which is said to contain the first poetiza-tion (in German literature) of skating.[2] Twenty years previously, however, Karl Ramler had written these verses in his poem *Sehnsucht nach dem Winter :* "Der Jüngling . . . . schweift Auf harten Wassern laut jauchzend umher, Die Füsse beschuhet mit Stahl, und überwindet den Reiter, Der am Gestade den Wettlauf gewagt." In his later odes Klopstock regrets his inability to skate, as we see from his poems, *Unterricht* (1781) and *Winterfreuden* (1797). He writes : "Also muss ich auf immer, Kristall der Ströme, dich meiden ? Darf nie wieder am Fuss schwingen die Flügel des Stahls? Wasserkothurn, du warst der Heilender einer . . . . ." His delight in skating he had expressed also in three other poems : *Braga* (1765), *Die Kunst Tialfs* (1767), and *Der Kamin* (1770). As we know from his life and letters that he was an enthusiastic skater, even when advanced in age, we can but con-clude that these odes did not take rise in his imagination, but were the outcome of his experiences. This holds true of many of his odes. It seems strange, on the other hand, that he should have passed by the Falls of the Rhine (see Letters) and not have left to posterity a poem embodying his feelings at sight of this extraordinary phenomenon, when men less gifted than he did not fail to poetize it.[3] Johann Kaspar Lavater, no doubt influenced by Klopstock's style, wrote from the castle of Laufen, in July, 1771, *Der Rheinfall bei Schaffhausen.* It begins :

[1] P. 28.   [2] Der Westen (Chicago), April 16, 1899.

[3] The only distinct reminiscence is in the long simile with which the ode *Aganippa und Phiala* (1764) opens.

Wer, wer gibt mir den Pinsel, wer Farben, dich zu entwerfen,
Grosser Gedanke der Schöpfung! Dich, majestätischer Rheinfall!
. . . . Schauernd staun' ich euch an, ihr rufenden Wogengewölke!
Ihr verschlingt mir den Odem, ihr raubt den Lippen die Stimme!
Unter dir zittert die Erde! Der Fels bebt! Prächtiger Aufruhr!

and closes with the lines:

Der Strom, der . . . . aus dem brausenden Aufschaum
Übertäubend dem Schauenden ruft, wie mit Stimmen der Meere:
"Gott ist! Herrlich ist Gott! ist Allmacht! Fühle dein Nichts hier!"

Klopstock, too, felt the presence of God everywhere, in the very flower
that blows, as he says in the ode *Dem Algegenwärtigen* (1758), and
hears His praise sounded by field and wood, dale and hill, shore and
sea (*Die Gestirne*, 1764).

Klopstock, as the author of the "Odes" and not of the "Messias," is
of the greatest importance in the history of the nature-sense. He sees
the external world with the eye of a poet, and describes it in language
appropriate to his theme; owing, however, to lack of close observation, his descriptions are seldom plastic. They often serve as starting-
points for eulogies on friendship, love, and other subjects. Unlike
the Anacreontics, he is interested in the sublime rather than the
humble aspects of nature. His nature-sense, of which the Odes are
the best index, grows somewhat stronger with approaching manhood,
and fainter after he has passed middle age, but withal we are scarcely
aware of any marked evolution. On the whole, he owes his importance
to the form rather than the content of his works.

THE BARDS.

Before turning to the first great modern writer, Herder, we wish to
speak briefly of the "Bardenpoesie," which had come in vogue with the
appearance of Wilhelm Gerstenberg's (1737–1823) *Gedicht eines Skalden*
(1766). Interest in Northern mythology had been on the increase for
some time, and had prepared the way for a favorable reception of the
magniloquent and turgid poetry of Macpherson. Thus it was that
Gerstenberg's poem with its Ossianic spirit aroused an audible echo,
not only in Klopstock's breast, but also in Kretschmann's, Denis's,
and others who became so infatuated with their bardic poetry that they
assumed strange-sounding names of imaginary bards, such as Rhingulf,
Sined, etc. Naturally their view of the external world became more or
less tinged with Ossianic magniloquence.

The second canto of Gerstenberg's poem contains a description of nature, typical of many to be found in the "Bardenpoesie." It begins thus : " Still war die Luft, in Majestät Lag die Natur zu Vidris Füssen ! Die stolzesten der Wipfel rauschten, Und leise Bäche murmelten . . . . Vom Hügel braust im Bogenschuss Ein breiter Quell, schwillt auf zum breitern Fluss, Springt donnernd über jähe Spitzen. . . . ." Similarly he pictures an ideal night (l. 63): " Die sternenvolle Nacht umschwebet sie, Die Flur ist Duft, der Wald ist Melodie. Sieh den gelinden West ihr Haar umfliessen ! O sieh den hellern Mond zu ihren Füssen ! " Not quite so unreal, and more Ossianic in spirit, are these lines of Canto 3 : " Einst da ich einsam und verlassen am Ufer irrt', und jeden Hauch der Luft, der nach der Küste blies, mit meinen Seufzern flügelte . . . ." Because of the lack of concreteness in the following passage of Canto 4, it is rather difficult to imagine with any degree of distinctness the landscape that the poet has in mind : " Wie reitzend, wie bezaubernd lacht Die heitre Gegend ! wie voll sanfter Pracht ! In schönrer Majestät, in reifer'm Strahle Glänzt diese Sonne ! Milder fliesst vom Thale Mir fremder Blüthen Frühlingsduft, Und Balsamgeister strömen durch die Luft. . . . ." In his frequently quoted drama, *Ugolino*, whose time of action is a stormy night, the background of nature is as unsatisfactory as the play itself. Only a few vague references to the weather are interspersed. In the fifth act, however, Ugolino exclaims with dramatic effect: " O nun beb', Erde ! nun brüllt, Stürme ! nun wimmre, Natur ! wimmre, Gebärerin ! wimmre ! wimmre ! die Stunde deines Kreisens ist eine grosse Stunde ! " This reminds one of the scene in King Lear (III : 2), and thus makes the inferiority of Gerstenberg's art even more evident.

Of the other bardic poets, Michael Denis (1729–1800) and Karl Friedrich Kretschmann (1738–1809) are best known. The former tries to describe a thunderstorm (*Das Gewitter*) in sixty-seven lines, but fails to impress us with the grandeur and majesty of this phenomenon. He cannot refrain from alluding to the gods of Northern mythology, and thus add a touch of unreality to his descriptions which by no means enhances their value. This is likewise true of his compeer, who tells us in *Ringulphs Gesang* (l. 79) how, as a boy, he was drawn to the forest: " Da horcht' ich oft am Wasserfall ; Ich lernte von der Nachtigall Am Abend, von der Lerche früh, Und selbst des Westwinds Melodie." And then continues : " Auch lausch ich oft bey Mondenglanz Auf den geheimnissvollen Tanz Der Jungfraun, welche sich im Hain Dem Dienst der schönen Freya weihn."

The range of observation of these "bards" is very small; their nature-sense is vague and emotional, but genuine. Their importance in the evolution of the poetry of nature is but slight.

JOHANN GOTTFRIED HERDER (1744–1803).

Next in importance to Klopstock's Odes in the history of the nature-sense, but of far wider reaching influence than they, are the works of Herder, both prose and verse. His all-important place in German literature he owes rather to the stimulating influence he exerted upon his contemporaries, and Goethe in particular, than to any distinct achievements of his own, though his prose works, not widely read nowadays, were in his time of the greatest possible consequence. He had come under the influence of English and French writers, of Macpherson and Percy, of Diderot and Rousseau, and caused in Germany a revival of folklore and a return to the natural way of expression, from which Klopstock's followers had drifted so far away. His epoch-making essay, "Ossian and the Songs of Ancient Nations" (1773), is a powerful protest against the artificiality of the eighteenth century, and emphasizes but more strongly the well-known words of Lessing: "Lebhafte Empfindungen sind nicht das Vorrecht gesitteter Völker."[1] In the folksongs he sees the same relationship existing as between the parts of nature, the trees and bushes, the rocks and grottoes. He read Ossian, as he tells us, in the midst of situations in which most people hardly ever read him — in mid-ocean, on his voyage to Nantes, in 1769 — "mitten im Schauspiel einer ganz andern lebenden und webenden Natur, zwischen Abgrund und Himmel schwebend, täglich mit denselben endlosen Elementen umgeben."[2]   Other reminiscences of his famous voyage can be traced in the *Unterhaltungen und Briefe über die ältesten Urkunden*, and especially in the *Älteste Urkunde des Menschengeschlechts* (1774). From the latter essay, some of the descriptions of which are said to have been suggested by Gessner's *Der Tod Abels*,[3] we shall quote at length, because of the truly poetic conception of nature contained in it. Herder compares the creation of the world to the beginning of day: "Wer jemals auf dem wüsten Weltmeer mit Nacht und Todesfurcht umhüllt auf Morgenröthe gehoft, wird diese Scene gefühlt haben — Geist des Himmels! Hauch Gottes! Wie er sich von droben her senkt, die Fluthen durchwühlt, emporwebt: wo er wandelt, webt. Himmlische Gegenwart: und alles ist Schauer!" He continues,

[1] Litteratur Briefe, no. 33.   [3] Suphan, Herders Werke, VI, Introduction, xii.
[2] Cf. Letters, p. 80.

with even greater inspiration (258): "Fühle den wehenden, durch-wehenden Nachtgeist, auch noch den Schauer der tiefsten Frühe vor Tagesanbruch, wie er Meer, Baum und alles durchnimmt — webender Geist Gottes auf der Tiefe! wer ists der nicht, unmittelbar vor Tages-anbruch, von ihm ergriffen, wie Gott, wie eine kommende Regkraft der Natur athme! . . . . Und siehe! diese Entzückung, dies unnenn-bare Morgengefühl, wies scheint alle Wesen zu ergreifen! zu liegen auf der ganzen Natur! . . . . Vielleicht die Blüthe des Baums, die Blume, die Knospe fühlen! Lichtstrahl! ein tönender Goldklang auf die grosse Laute der Natur — die Lerche erwacht und schwingt sich — wehe dem Fühllosen, der diese Scene gesehn und Gott nicht gefühlt hat!" Now darkness gives way to light, and the earth, like a huge mountain, rises up, casting off her veil. Flowers and trees feel the approach of the morning air. Then the sun appears in all his glory and majesty: "Das Auge kann nur Einen Anblick aushalten! Übertrift und endet alles!" Water and air are filled with life. "Alles voll Regung, Gesang, Freude und Segen!" A description in prose, yet how poetic! Only one who had observed a complete sunrise could draw such a picture.

In his other early prose works Herder has but little to say of nature. Of interest are only his comments upon the elegy, which should have as a background the banks of a sadly flowing stream, for-ests, rocks, "wo die Aussicht und Stille in der Seele die Vorstellung der Gefahr und das Bewusstseyn der Sicherheit wechselsweise hervor-bringen."[1] He himself enjoyed reading Young's "Night Thoughts," and Creuz's "Die Gräber," never so much as on certain summer nights under a starry heaven in the silent arbor of his garden, which adjoined a graveyard, "wo alte heilige Linden, vom Hauche der Nacht beseelt, Schauder in die Seele rauschten, und aus den etwas entferntern Trüm-mern eines sinkenden ritterlichen Schlosses . . . . die Philosophische Eule ihre hole Accente manchmal darunter stiess."[2]

We shall see in another chapter (Letters) "dass in jenen farben-prächtigen Schilderungen" — which we quoted from the *Urkunde* —"das Naturgefühl Herders hervorbricht, das, wohl auch früher sanfter Schwärmerei und Entzückung fähig, ... in der patriarcha-lischen Einsamkeit dieser Jahre (1772–1776) seine Blüte voll entfaltet."[3]

[1] *Fragmente*, III, 3, III.

[2] Ibid. footnote.—In *Kritische Wälder* (II, 9) he says: "Ausserordentlich wilde Gegenden, Wüsten, Gebirge, Wasserfälle sind rührend, aber nur so fern sie bekannte Ideen wecken, die uns schon beiwohnen."

[3] Suphan, loc. cit.

This difference is perceptible also in his poems. Compare, for example, the poems *Ein Landlied auf Gravenheide* and *Die Dämmerung*, of the years 1766 and 1769 respectively, with the poems *Erdbeeren* and *St. Johanns Nachtstraum*, of the year 1772, and it becomes apparent that, though the earlier ones also testify to his genuine love and observation of nature, they are yet not equal in depth and power of description to the later ones. A few lines of the *Landlied* run thus: " O Natur ! du glänzest unerschöpflich reich ; und ein Ort den du bekränzest lacht der Kunst und des Gepränges, und ist Eden gleich . . . . Wenn in Abendroth der Himmel schwimmt, wähl ich dich, o See ! Wenn der Silberthau auf Wiesen glimmt, wähl ich dich, Allee !" How much more impressive and pulsating with the very life in nature are the lines of *St. Johanns Nachtstraum:* " Schönste Sommernacht ! Ich schwimm in Rosen und blühenden Bohnen und Blumen und Hecken und Nachtviolen, in tausend Düften ! — O Mutter Natur, wo kenn' ich deine Kinder alle, ... die jetzt sich schmücken und lieben und paaren und Freude duften in der schönsten Brautnacht ! . . . . Unendlich ach ! Unerschöpflich bist du schön ! Mutter Natur !" Equally significant are the verses of the poem *Erdbeeren*. In none of Herder's predecessors have we found a personification equal to the following in accuracy of observation, or aptness of expression : " Wie sie dort im Grase Hügelaufwärts glühen Und ins Grün erröthen ! Jetzt den Wanderer lieblich locken, jetzt entschlüpfet täuschen — Bulerinnen wie die Erdentöchter ! "

Of Herder's other poems previous to his removal to Weimar only two concern us here : one in which he compares Luther to the sturdy oak that, in spite of the fiercest storms, stands firmly rooted, and the other in which he notes the beautiful song of the invisible lark.[1] Two of his very best efforts, *Parthenope* and *Angedenken an Neapel,* do not come within the scope of this treatise because of their late date (1789).[2]

Herder, as from other points of view, is also from ours the first modern. He speaks of nature as does one who has closely observed her and genuinely loves her; though often in prose his descriptions are as poetic as any in the literature of the eighteenth century. His range of observation is much wider than that of his predecessors; he sees beauty in the small and the great things of nature, and knows how to interpret it. Even the grandeur of the ocean he appreciates, as we shall see in the chapter on letters. Here, for the first time, we feel the necessity of treating the works and letters together : they are the expression of one and the same spirit.

[1] Werke, XXIX, 53, 390.   [2] Nor should Winter have quoted them (32).

THE GÖTTINGER HAINBUND.

Herder's influence was soon to rival and finally to surpass Klopstock's. Some of their followers, men younger than they, students at
the University of Göttingen, came together on September 12, 1772,
and formed the Hainbund. A few others poetically inclined soon
joined them, or established a fairly close relationship with them. Next
to Goethe it is due to this whole group that German lyric poetry
became once more "in Empfindung und Gestaltung schlicht und innig,
natürlich und ursprünglich, ächt deutsch und volksthümlich."[1] We
shall speak of them in the following order, beginning with the poet
who is least important for the present purpose : Voss, Bürger, Claudius,
Hölty, and Friedrich Stolberg.

JOHANN HEINRICH VOSS (1751–1826).

Voss, the scholar of the Hainbund, contributed only a few poems,
before the appearance of Werther, that are of interest to us. His most
significant lines, *Der Winter* (1771), strike us as strange, because of
their meter, and are devoid of that broad sympathy for nature that
characterizes the productions of some of his contemporaries. He says
of winter : "Graunvoll tummelt er Nachtgewölk Durch aufbrausendes
Meer, krachende Waldung durch : Weiss dann wirbelt die Flur ; und
schnell Harscht der Bach, und im See heulet gediegner Frost." The
poet manifests no genuine appreciation of this season, but, like so many
of his predecessors, prefers a cozy seat by the chimney-fire where he
can enjoy a pleasant chat.

GOTTFRIED AUGUST BÜRGER (1747–94).

Of greater importance by far are Bürger's poems, though they too
show some affiliations with preceding schools of poetry, especially with
the Anacreontic. Bürger prefers the singing of his sweetheart to al
the concerts of larks and nightingales, and bids the wind and th
brook be his messengers to her, or witnesses of his tender affection fo
her.[2] The arrival of spring he pictures rather graphically :

> Unter frohen Melodieen
> Ist der junge Lenz erwacht.
> Seht wie Stirn und Wang' ihm glühen,
> Wie sein helles Auge lacht ![3]

[1] Hettner, Litgesch., III, I, 294.
[2] *Die beiden Liebenden; An ein Maienlüftchen; Das harte Mädchen.*
[3] *Die Nachtfeier der Venus; Danklied.*

The description of his little village, with its fields of corn and its meadows, and in the distance the blue woods, is well known. Besides these features he sees the following: "Dort kränzen Schlehen Die braune Kluft, Und Pappeln wehen In blauer Luft. Mit sanftem Rieseln Schleicht hier gemach Auf Silberkieseln Ein heller Bach."[1] With only these references at hand one would be justified in classing him with the idyllic poets. When, however, the poem *Lenore* (1773), in which nature is used with consummate skill as a background for the action, is taken into account, such classification will seem not quite just. The deft use of nature in this poem is proof positive that his place is among the best of modern poets. The frequent repetition of "Der Mond scheint hell" at different points of the wild midnight ride intensifies the already weird atmosphere of the ballad. The reader feels the rough air of this evil-boding night when he hears: "Den Hagedorn durchsaust der Wind," and can image vividly the peculiar noise of the spirits rushing headlong on, when the poet says of it: "Wie Wirbelwind am Haselbusch Durch dürre Blätter rasselt." Lastly, the mention of the fluttering ravens and the croaking of the frogs helps to create "the atmosphere of lurid mystery which hovers about it."

As already observed, we should class Bürger with the idyllic poets, were it not for his skilful and dramatic use of nature in *Lenore*. This poem was in more than one respect of the greatest importance in the subsequent history of German poetry.

MATTHIAS CLAUDIUS (1740–1815).

As simple, sincere, and "volkstümlich" as Bürger is Matthias Claudius, the editor of the "Wandsbecker Bothen." His poems, which show genuine love and first-hand observation of nature, are no doubt based on his own experience. Well might he have written such poems as *Morgenlied eines Bauernmanns* ("Da kommt die liebe Sonne wieder") or *Abendlied* ("Der Mond ist aufgegangen") as he was driving through the country and observing with an appreciative eye the manifold aspects of nature. Thus he tells his readers on Good Friday morning in a simple and straightforward way: "Bin die vorige Nacht unterwegen gewesen. Etwas kalt schien der Mond auf den Leib, sonst war er aber so hell und schön, dass ich recht meine Freude dran hatt', und mich an ihm nicht konnte satt sehen." Then he meditates: "Heut Nacht vor tausend acht hundert Jahren schienst du gewiss nicht so; denn es war

[1] *Das Dörfchen.*

doch wohl nicht möglich, dass Menschen im Angesicht eines so freundlichen sanften Mond's einen gerechten unschuldigen Mann Leid thun konnten!"[1] Elsewhere he addresses the moon even more familiarly, and in a humorous way confesses his love for her when a boy: "Ich pflegt' in den Wald zu laufen und halbverstohlen hinter'n Bäumen nach Ihnen umzublicken, wenn Sie mit blosser Brust oder im Negligee einer zerrissenen Nachtwolke vorübergiengen."[2] He is fond of both spring and winter, and likes to sing of them equally well, as the following verses demonstrate:

> Sieh! der Frühling kommt nun wieder,
> Und die Nachtigall, ...
> Und wir singen Frühlingslieder,
> Und dann fallen in den Schall
> Tausend weisse Blüthen nieder.[3]

* * * * * * *

> Der Winter ist ein rechter Mann,
> Kernfest und auf die Dauer;
> Sein Fleisch fühlt sich wie Eisen an,
> Und scheut nicht Süss noch Sauer.[4]

At heart he probably prefers spring, for he tells his readers in June: "So 'n heller Decembertag is auch wohl schön und dankenswerth, wenn Berg und Thal in Schnee gekleidet sind, und uns Bothen in der Morgenstunde der Bart bereift; aber die Lenzgestalt der Natur ist doch wunderschön! Und die Welt hat Blätter, und der Vogel singt, und die Saat schiesst Aehren, und dort hängt die Wolke mit dem Bogen vom Himmel, und der fruchtbare Regen rauscht herab." Then the poet sings for very joy: "Wach auf mein Herz und singe Dem Schöpfer aller Dinge . . . . 's ist, als ob Er vorüber wandle, und die Natur habe Sein Kommen von Ferne gefühlt und stehe bescheiden am Weg' in ihrem Feyerkleid, und frolocke!"[5] He believes he has every reason for thanking God who has given him the privilege "die Sonne, Berg und Meer Und Laub und Gras [zu] sehn, und Abends unterm Sternenheer Und lieben Monde gehen."[6]

Sincerity and genuineness are characteristics of Claudius's nature-sense. His observations are first-hand, but do not comprehend the more romantic aspects of nature, although he no doubt had the opportunity of seeing them.

---

[1] *Der Wandsbecker Bothen: Am Charfreitagmorgen* (Pt. I, 8).
[2] *Ein Brief an den Mond* (Pt. I, 120).   [4] *Ein Lied hinterm Ofen zu singen* (Pt. IV, 141).
[3] *Als Daphne krank war* (Pt. I, 200).   [5] *Im Junius* (Pt. I, 50).   [6] *Täglich zu singen* (Pt. III,128).

LUDWIG HEINRICH CHRISTIAN HÖLTY (1748–76).

The nature-sense of Hölty has many points in common with that of Claudius, except in the later years of his brief life, when the melancholy, which seized Hölty, affected to a considerable extent his view of nature. He loved the country where he had spent his youth and, owing to the impressions he received there, he became a poet of nature and of country life almost exclusively. Unlike the poems of previous decades, his songs are the genuine expression of his feelings, and, as Karl Halm states it: "Da der schwärmerische Hang, in der Natur zu schwelgen, ihn auch in den späteren Jahren seines Lebens nicht verliess, so spricht sich in allen Naturschilderungen und ländlichen Liedern ein lauteres, ungekünsteltes Gefühl aus, dem man es leicht anmerkt, dass das Herz wirklich mitgesungen hat."[1] Many of his poems were in fact composed in the country, "im lieblichen Mai, unter blühenden Bäumen und Nachtigallen," as Hölty writes in a letter to Voss,[2] and fondly hopes that they may breathe "etwas von der Maienanmuth, die von allen Seiten auf mich zuströmte, als ich sie sang." His wish was fulfilled, for his songs would not be heard to this very day, if they had not something of the "Maienanmuth" in them.

Beginning with 1771 he wrote every year one or more poems in praise of spring and May, some of which form today a part of the stock-in-trade of editors of school readers and anthologies. We note these in chronological order: 1771, *Mailied* ("Tanzt den schönen Mai entgegen"); 1772, "Heil dir, lächelnder Mai, Blumenschöpfer, Herzenfessler," and "Schön im Feierschmucke lächelt Hold und bräutlich die Natur;" 1773 (his most productive year), "Willkommen liebe Sommerzeit,— Grün wird Wies' und Au . . . . Jedes Haingesträuch Flüstert freuet euch!— Der Schnee zerrinnt, Der Mai beginnt— Die Luft ist blau, das Thal ist grün, die kleinen Maienglocken blühn;" 1774, "Wenn der silberne Mond durch die Gesträuche blickt;" 1775, *Trinklied im Mai;* and 1776, "Röther schimmert der Morgen." No comment is necessary, for they are well-known to everyone who is at all familiar with German lyric poetry. The poet of spring misses, of course, in winter birds and flowers (*Winterlied*, 1773), thus showing that in this respect he has not gone beyond the majority of poets before him.

Next in importance to the spring songs are those addressed to the moon. Though it may be possible, yet it is not probable, that they

---

[1] Höltys Gedichte, Einl., xxix.   [2] Mariensee, June 12, 1775.

were inspired by the reading of Young and Ossian. It has been said above that a few years before his death Hölty grew melancholy, and like a true poet he recorded in his songs his various moods. In 1771 he still could write: "Schon als hüpfender Knabe. . . . sass ich am Wiesenbach Und beschaute dein Antlitz [Mond] Mit verschlingendem Wonneblick."[1] Only two years later his joy has changed to discontent: "Wann itzt dein Licht Durchs Fenster bricht, Lacht's keine Ruh Mir Jüngling zu."[2] His thoughts are centered on death: "Wann, lieber Freund, Ach wann bescheint Dein Silberschein Den Leichenstein, Der meine Asche birgt?" The following year he asks of the moon aid and sympathy: "Enthülle dich, dass ich des Strauchs mich freue, Der Kühling ihr gerauscht. . . . Dann, lieber Mond, dann nimm den Schleier wieder Und traur' um deinen Freund."[3] The complete change that had come over him is distinctly marked in his pronounced tendency to address the moon rather than the sun, as he had done in the earlier part of his short career, when he poured forth this superb ode:

> Heil dir, Mutter des Lichts! Sie bestrahlet den Hain,
> Der vom Fittich des Winds auf dem Gebirge nickt . . . .
> Wie der Puls der Natur jetzt so jugendlich klopft!
> Wie des Waldes Musik von den Wipfeln ertönt![4]

Hölty's poems, also, are the expression of genuine and deep-felt emotion. We have sufficient evidence to believe that he gained his knowledge of nature from actual observation. His spring songs, which are justly famous because of their simplicity and naturalness, breathe the air of outdoor life, while his poems to the moon are filled with a melancholy spirit.

FRIEDRICH LEOPOLD STOLBERG (1750–1819).

Friedrich Stolberg, who from our point of view is the most important poet of the Hainbund, differs from all other members of this group in his intense love of the grand and sublime in nature, and in his ability to embody his feelings in apt and poetic language. He had from his very youth, as Scherer says,[5] "ein tiefes Bedürfnis, zu verehren, ... sei es Homer oder die Natur, sei es die Heldenkraft unserer Ahnen oder das Meer." Stolberg did not want anyone as a friend who did not love nature, for "Schauer begegneten, In hoher

---

[1] *Hymnus an den Mond.*   [3] *An den Mond,* 1774.
[2] *An den Mond.*   [4] *Hymnus an die Morgensonne,* 1771.   [5] Litgesch., 507.

Wallung, seiner Seele Nie mit der steigenden Morgensonne" (*Die Natur*, 1773). He voiced most perfectly the dominant feeling in the seventies when he wrote, after seeing the Falls of the Rhine, those frequently quoted lines :

> Süsse, heilige Natur !
> Lass mich gehn auf deiner Spur.
> Leite mich an deiner Hand,
> Wie ein Kind am Gängelband !—*An die Natur*, 1775.

It was to nature that Homer owed his greatness, as Stolberg says in his ode to the ancient bard : " Es liebte dich früh Die heilige Natur ! . . . . Weihte dich und säugte dich an ihrer Brust ! " [1]

The poet had spent his boyhood in close proximity to the sea, had grown fond of it (see Letters), and in his manhood sang of the grandeur of the ocean over and over again — the ocean which up to his time had played no conspicuous part in German poetry,[2] and had to wait for adequate treatment in English literature for Byron and Shelley.[3] As one reads his apostrophes to the sea, the earliest of which were composed in the year 1777, one feels that they are imbued throughout with the modern spirit and could have been written only by one whose home was by the sea. His best-known ode begins thus :

> Du heiliges und weites Meer,
> Wie ist dein Anblick mir so hehr !
> Sei mir im frühen Strahl gegrüsst,
> Der zitternd deine Lippen küsst ! . . . .
> Wann sich zu dir die Sonne neigt,
> Erröthend in dein Lager steigt,
> Dann tönet deiner Wogen Klang
> Der müden Erde Wiegensang.[4]

Klopstock's intense delight in skating is surely equaled by Stolberg's exuberant joy in bathing in the ocean's waves, for he continues his apostrophe to the ocean thus :

> Oft eil ich aus der Haine Ruh',
> Mit Wonne deinen Wogen zu,
> Und senke mich hinab in dich,
> Und kühle, labe, stärke mich.

This same entering into the very arms of the ocean, as it were, he expresses even more strongly in the *Badelied* (1777):

1 *Homer*, 1775.   3 Reynolds, Treatment of Nature, etc., 256.
2 Keiper, F. L. Stolbergs Jugendpoesie, 48.   4 *An das Meer.* Cf. *Hymne an die Erde*, 1778.

O rühmliche Wonne,
Mit Mond und mit Sonne
Zu baden im Meer!
Die wallenden Gluthen
Der purpurnen Fluthen
So rund um uns her!

The siren song of the swashing waves entices him to sink into the very lap of the sea: "Du schmeichelst meinem Ohr, Ich kenne dein Rauschen, Deiner Wogen Sirenengesang! Ostsee, du nahmst mich oft mit schmeichelnden Armen In den kühlenden Schooss!" (*Die Meere*, 1777). At other times he wanders at midnight to the ocean to seek inspiration from the billowy sea, and the swelling waves, and the shimmering stars,[1] for they all are his friends; he speaks of the ocean, the earth, and the heaven as "traulich und hold."[2] Not until many years later do we find such genuine love and appreciation of the ocean.[3]

Not less significant than his treatment of the ocean is his use of the mountain torrent. Up to his time, and especially with the Anacreontic poets, the purling brook was the usual emblem of life. Not so with Stolberg. He likens his life and his brother's to "Zwillingsströme, [die] sich hell stürzen von Felsen herab, Mit vereinter Kraft bald Tannen wälzen und Felsen," or compares a band of heroes to the Rhine "[der] von jähen Felsen herab Seine Donner stürzet und ewigen Schaum, Mit des Adlers Eile, des Meeres Schall."[4] It is entirely modern in spirit when he no longer draws his metaphors from nature, but looks upon her elements as if they were human beings. This we shall see presently in his references to the Hartz and the moon, but can also note in his poem *Der Felsenstrom* (1775), composed near the Wallenstädter See and perhaps influenced by Goethe's Mahomets Gesang.[5] It begins thus: "Unsterblicher Jüngling! Du strömest hervor Aus der Felsenkluft. . . . . Wie bist du so furchtbar Im Donner der hallenden Felsen umher! . . . . Du stürzest die Tanne mit Wurzel und Haupt!" Like the torrent, the whirlpool and the storm are looked upon as companions.[6]

As we have indicated elsewhere (p. 41), Stolberg is the first to appreciate poetically the beauty of the Hartz and during his sojourn in Göttingen[7] wrote these splendid lines:

---

[1] *Hellebeck eine Seeländische Gegend*, 1776.   [2] *Der Abend*, 1783.   [3] Cf. Walzel, Euphorion, V, 154.
[4] *Elegie an meinen Bruder*, 1778; *Freiheitsgesang*, 1775.   [5] Scherer, Anz. f. d. Alt., II, 284.
[7] Here he also composed *An die Weende von Göttingen*, 1773.   [6] *Lied eines Freigeistes*, 1776.

> Herzlich sei mir gegrüsst, werthes Cheruskaland! . . . .
> Dir gab Mutter Natur . . . . Einfalt und Würde!
> Wolkenhöhnende Gipfel, donnerhallende Ströme dir! . . . .
> Wie der schirmende Forst deinem erhabenen Nacken schattet! [1]

In his *Freiheitsgesang* (1775) he sees the indications of Germany's future greatness, just as he sees in the early morning the indications of the full beauty of the Brocken at midday : "Wie der Brocken stolz, wenn der Morgenröthe Licht Seine Scheitel röthet, noch finster unter ihm liegen die Thale, und nur dämmern die Gipfel um ihn her!"

Lastly we should add a few words concerning his treatment of the moon and of winter. He attributes human qualities to the moon, when he imagines her to be sad, because some friend has departed, "Schied dir ein Freund, o Mond? Du blickst so traurig Durch die hangenden Maien!" and as he thinks of his mother he wonders whether the moon, too, "denkt an sie zurück." [2] His attitude toward winter is even more noteworthy, for, with the exception of Brockes and Klopstock, none of his predecessors recorded the charms of this season ; and even of these two it can hardly be said that they fully appreciated a winter landscape. Stolberg, as his letters show,[3] observed it, appreciated it, and described it in his *Winterlied* (1776):

> Auch sieht mich alles freundlich an
> Im Schmuck des Winters angethan,
> Das Meer, gepanzert, weiss und hart,
> Der krause Wald, der blinkend starrt.

He loved nature in all her manifold aspects, but, unlike Brockes, not as a manifestation of God, but for her own sake. And thus he cries :

> Natur, du wirst mir nimmer alt
> In deiner wechselnden Gestalt!
> Natur so hehr! so wunderbar!
> Und doch so traut! und doch so wahr! (Ibid.)

Though the other poets of the Hainbund contributed largely to a better and more genuine appreciation of nature than had been current among their predecessors, Friedrich Stolberg deserves the lion share of the credit. Coupled with the power of close observation and intense love for the grand and terrible in nature is the ability to interpret

---

[1] *Der Harz*, 1772. The thoughts that arose in Goethe on his visit to the same mountains are poetically embodied in the famous *Harzreise im Winter*, 1777.

[2] *An den Mond*, 1773; *Der Mond*, 1775.   [3] To Catherine, Oct. 14 and Nov. 22, 1777.

poetically. Unlike preceding writers, his eyes are not holden to the charms of winter or the grandeur of mountains and sea; nay, he verily revels in them, though not quite in the spirit of his contemporary, Goethe. This one, as we shall see presently, is to give the fullest and most felicitous expression to the new feeling for nature.

JOHANN WOLFGANG GOETHE (1749–1832).

As we read Friedrich Stolberg's poems we hear notes which are unmistakably a prelude to the grand symphony about to be played. The time had arrived when a genius of the highest order was to interpret nature, as she had never been interpreted before. In the very beginning, to be sure, a greater or less dependence on his immediate predecessors is easily traceable in his lyrics, but even in them indications of a greater genius are not wanting. Ere long he furnished proof indisputable that he was the poet of nature par excellence.

Even in his earliest verses Goethe's use of metaphors and similes is remarkable.[1] As was the fashion among literary men of his day, he intersperses poetry in his letters. Thus he writes to his friend Riese (Leipzig, Dec. 21, 1765): "Ich lebe so ungefähr So wie ein Vogel, der auf einem Ast Im schönsten Wald sich Freiheit atmend wiegt. Der ungestört die sanfte Luft geniesst, Mit seinen Fittichen von Baum zu Baum, von Busch zu Busch, sich singend hinzuschwingen." Elsewhere he compares his heart, full of peace and joy, to the lightest cloud that floats serenely above him, and the joy of stealing a kiss seems to him like that of picking a violet in March.[2]

His early lyrics were, no doubt, influenced by the Anacreontics. He, too, loves to lie by the side of a brook and meditate,[3] and compose his songs,[4] and enjoy the rolling waves :

> Im spielenden Bache da lieg ich wie helle !
> Verbreite die Arme der kommenden Welle,
> Und buhlerisch drückt sie die sehnende Brust.
> Dann trägt sie ihr Leichtsinn im Strome darnieder,
> Schon naht sich die Zweyte und streichelt mich wieder,
> Da fühl ich die Freuden der wechselnden Lust.[5]

The best-known song of these " Leipziger Lieder," and, in many respects, one superior to any in the collection, is entitled *Die Nacht*. Barring a few expressions which show the influence of the Anacreontic poets, the poem is permeated by a spirit unknown to that school. With

---

[1] Cf. Victor Hehn, Gedanken über Goethe, chap. vi.   [2] Bernays, Der junge Goethe, I, 108, 112.
[3] Letter to Riese, April 28, 1766.   [4] Cf. *Zuneigung.*   [5] Der junge Goethe, I, 104.

a few sure touches the poet makes us feel the charms of the night ("schöne, süsse Nacht"). The poem was written, however, before Goethe's sojourn at Strassburg, and the consequent change (or sloughing, as R. M. Meyer calls it) which was brought about chiefly through Herder's influence. *Die Nacht* might well be compared, as Scherer has so excellently suggested,[1] to his song *An Friederike:* "Es schlug mein Herz, geschwind zu Pferde," which was composed only two or three years later. It is needless to quote it here, or to comment upon it, as it is universally known and has been analyzed and annotated by the foremost critics; it were perhaps better to say a word in regard to another poem, written about the same time and equally well-known, *Mayfest* (1771), "Wie herrlich leuchtet mir die Natur." And this, despite V. Hehn,[2] who passes over it, because it consists, as he says, only of exclamations current since Hagedorn, and might have been composed equally well by Gleim, Uz, or J. G. Jacobi. In our study of these men we confess to have found no verses that can be put side by side with these of Goethe's. Such exuberance of feeling, such a superb yet natural way of expression, are well-nigh foreign to them.

Goethe had now altogether broken with the Anacreontic traditions, and no longer hesitated to publish his manifesto. In his review of J. G. Sulzer's *Die schönen Künste* (1771) he says : "Gehört denn, was unangenehme Eindrücke auf uns macht, nicht so gut in den Plan der Natur als ihr Lieblichstes ? Sind die wüthenden Stürme, Wasserfluthen Feuerregen . . . . nicht eben so wahre Zeugen ihres ewigen Lebens, als die herrlich aufgehende Sonne ? . . . . Was wir von Natur sehn, ist Kraft, die Kraft verschlingt, nichts gegenwärtig, alles vorübergehend, tausend Keime zertreten, jeden Augenblick tausend gebohren, gross und bedeutend, mannigfaltig ins Unendliche."[3] This is the spirit which now pervades his poems. Compare *Der Wanderer, Wanderers Sturmlied, Gesang nach Mahomet, Rastlose Liebe*, etc. At the same time he perceives the kinship of the spirit of nature with the spirit of man. His love of nature grows more intense, and he sings : "Wie ist Natur so hold und gut, Die mich am Busen hält." As he glides along on the water, he observes her manifold aspects : "Auf der Welle blinken Tausend schwebende Sterne, Weiche Nebel trinken Rings die thürmende Ferne, Morgenwind umflügelt Die beschattete Bucht, Und im See bespiegelt Sich die reifende Frucht."[4]

Not only in joy, but in sorrow as well, he turns to nature, and though she, too, is sad, she is yet more hopeful than he, as the following

---

[1] Litgesch., 481.   [2] Loc. cit., 307.   [3] Der junge Goethe, II, 472.   [4] Ibid., III, 182.

verses show : " Ein zärtlich jugendlicher Kummer Führt mich in's öde Feld, es liegt In einem stillen Morgenschlummer Die Mutter Erde, rauschend wiegt Ein kalter Wind die starren Aeste. Schauernd tönt er die Melodie zu meinem Lied voll Schmerz. Und die Natur ist ängstlich still und trauernd, Doch hoffnungsvoller als mein Herz."[1] Such close correspondence between the moods of man and nature will be presently seen delineated with greater skill and dramatic effect in *Werther*.[2]

First, however, it may be well to pass in review the novels before the appearance of *Werther*, to determine the part that nature plays in them. In England, the home of the modern novel, there is not found in the works of fiction before 1756 "a single passage indicating any close observation or love of nature," and even after that date " development is spasmodic and slow."[3] Smollett's "Humphrey Clinker" (1771) is probably the first novel permeated by the new spirit. In how far English fiction was influenced by Rousseau's "Nouvelle Heloïse" (1761) Miss Reynolds does not tell us. In Germany this famous novel, which for the first time opened the eyes of many readers and writers to the world of nature, left its distinct impress on *Fräulein von Sternheim*, (1771), and especially *Werther* (1774).[4] In the preceding works of fiction, the " Abenteuer und Schelmenromane," beginning with *Simplicissimus* (1668), and including *Insel Felsenburg* (1731–43), occasional references to nature are found.[5] Not as much can be said of some of the novels which followed in historical sequence, which, faithful to their prototypes, the works of Richardson and Fielding, almost totally ignored the external world. Compare, for example, Gellert's *Das Leben der schwedischen Gräfin v. G.*, 1746. Mention has been made above of the comparatively slight use of nature in Wieland's novels, for, though he considers the direct impressions of the majestic spectacle of nature the prime source of " Ausschweifungen der Schwärmerei,"[6] still the use of nature in his works hardly substantiates this claim.

In Thümmel's *Wilhelmine* (1764) there are a few scattered nature-references, contained mostly in curious similes, of which the following may serve as illustration : "Thränen der Freude rollten über seinen stachlichten Bart herunter, wie ein plötzlicher Sommerregen über die

[1] D. j. G., I, 271.   [3] Reynolds, Treatment of Nature, etc., 217, 229.

[2] Only few references to nature are found in *Götz von Berlichingen*, the most striking perhaps in the last scene, where Götz, before dying, enjoys his last moments in the open air. Cf. R. M. Meyer, Goethe, 86.

[4] E. Schmidt, Richardson, Rousseau und Goethe, 57, 133, 173, et passim.

[5] Winter, Beiträge z. Gesch. d. Naturgefühls, 23.   [6] *Don Sylvio* (1764), Book I, ch. 3.

glänzenden Stoppeln der Felder " (4. Gesang). There is certainly a vein
of humor running through Thümmel's description of the rising sun on
a New Year's morning : " Ihr ungewohnter Blick übersah schüchtern
die Planeten. . . . . Betäubt von den murrenden Wünschen der Thor-
heit und von den lauten Seufzern des Unglücks, stund die Sonne in
wehmüthiger Schönheit am Himmel, fürchtete sich länger herab zu
schauen, und versteckte sich oft hinter ein trübes Gewölke" (2. Gesang).
    The sequel to this book, Nicolai's *Sebaldus Nothanker* (1773),
makes larger and better use of nature, especially in the second and
third parts (1775–76), with which this study is, however, less concerned.
In Part I love of nature is evident, but chiefly as found in parks and
gardens.   The countess preferred the beauties of nature to the pomp
of court (230), and did not refrain from walking on beautiful winter
days (II, 144).   Marianne's protégée, Adelheid, often stole into the
garden to see the setting sun, to hear the nightingales, and to inhale
the odor of gillyflower and jasmin (I, 177).   Marianne's lover, Säug-
ling, exclaims : " Meine Seele ist zu voll, als dass ich die Schönheiten der Natur empfinden könnte " (I, 214), and then compares himself to a violet, and her to the sun without whose power the violet
cannot bloom.   He goes out into nature to plan, " unter den Einflüs-
sen der schönen Gegend," a scene of his novel (III, 125).   And Marianne strolls about in the early hours of the morning to imbibe the
beauties of the charming country, and to find her lover's image mir-
rored in every leaf and bud (III, 104, 108).   Her father, Sebaldus, is
indeed a lover of nature.   He regards with pleasure the dense foliage
of chestnut trees, but ignores the castle on the way (II, 22).   He sees
" die glückliche Mischung dunkler Fichten mit schlanken Ulmen,
hellgrünen weissrindigen Birken, und glatten Akacien unterbrochen,
denen hundertjährige majestätische Eichen zum Hintergrunde dienen,
[und] melancholische Gänge von dichtem Lerchenholze, und von
düstern Eichenbäumen."   He is refreshed by the odor of pines and of
"Lindenblüthe," is charmed by a walk on a beautiful autumn day, and
even when in adversity delights in the view of land and sea.[1]
    In the ten volumes of *Sophiens Reise* (Hermes), published 1769–
73, there are scattered references to the external world, most of
them pertaining to a sunrise, or a sunset.   In one of the first letters
(I, 28) Sophie regrets that the charms of morning have been so often
described, for she would like to picture them, and then she proceeds to

[1] II, 23, 24, 50; III, 48. In this as in the following novel, Carl Heine (Der Roman in Deutschland, 123, 119) notes only one reference to nature.

depict them. Other characters, like Prof. T. (IV, 22), and Julchen (VI, 94), are also delighted with a sunrise which they think no poet can describe with justice, and Johanne looks back " mit Thränen der Sehnsucht" to the lake in which the village is reflected in the morning sunshine (V.I, 355). Evening, too, has its charms for Sophie (I, 85). She listens intently to the song of the nightingale and the imitative "Rohrsperling," but, fearing that she gives vent to her feelings too strongly, she says: "doch ich rede hievon wol gar mit Schwärmerei ?" (I, 38). Occasionally she feels in sympathy with nature: "Die ganze Gegend um mich her, ein See unter meinem Fenster, der Wald, die Luft, und ich—alles ist still" (I, 127). When she is enjoying a trip on the Baltic sea during a beautiful autumn evening, she feels sorry that there is no sensitive soul on board to share the pleasure with her. The moon seems to look down at her with compassion. "Auf der pommerschen Küste," she writes, "macht der so benannte weisse Berg eine unvergleichliche Würkung gegen die schwarze See, und gegen die vielfarbige Landschaft, und das alles schliesst sich hinten an den hellen Himmel mit dem sanften Grau der Waldungen" (VIII, 37). There may be added one comment on autumn which anticipates a thought in *Werther*. "Der Herbst," says one of the letter-writers, "hat von jeher etwas von einer süssen Schwermuth für mich gehabt" (II, 138).

Much less is said of nature in Haller's political novel *Usong* (1771), the scene of which is laid in Persia. Large gardens, beautiful brooks, gaily colored flowers, etc., are merely mentioned (14, 112, 184), but lack of skill in description is evident throughout the book. In accordance with tradition, mountains are designated as "öde," "beschwerlich," "unwegsam" (111, 185, etc.).

An altogether different spirit toward nature prevails in an anonymous story which appeared in the same year as the "Nouvelle Heloïse," 1761, entitled *Die Reise auf die Gebürge*. Such enthusiasm for nature as is here manifested may not be found in any previous work, and, what is more, genuine love and close observation of wild, free nature are expressed in a thoroughly modern way. Our ignorance as to its authorship is to be lamented, for it is probable that the identity of the author might reveal much of interest to the student of the nature-sense. As this short story is so little known, some unusually long extracts may be of value:

Lange hat dein Pamelon nicht solch Vergnügen geschmeckt, als da er nun am schönen Sommerabende mit seinen Freunden die Reise auf die

Gebürge antrat. Ein milder Regen begünstigte unser Vorhaben, denn nach dem Regen verjüngte die Natur sich, und alle Felder und Wiesen und Auen dufteten balsamisch. Der Mond schien der Natur an diesem Tage auch die minutenlange Ruhe nicht zu gönnen, die die Sonne ihr liess. Wie schön ist diese Gegend im Mondscheine! (sagte Menalkas). Sehet, wie über jene Ebene der Schatten hinläuft, als flöhe er vor uns zu den Gebürgen hinauf! Hinter uns stehen Tempel und Thürme mit veränderten Gestalten, und scheinen wie Phantome in der Luft zu tanzen (8, 9). Schon wurde das Erdreich uneben, und wir stiegen bergan, da lief Strephon aus allen Kräften voraus, um zuerst auf dem Gipfel des Berges zu seyn: und da er ihn erreicht hatte, stellte er sich auf einen Stein hin, and schrie herunter: hier, Freunde, ist die paradiesische Gegend, denn hier ist die Erde weit schöner denn unten. .... Da kamen wir durch dicke Wälder von Eichen, deren Boden in ewigem Schatten liegt, und deren Innerstes nur von alten Hirschen oder gejagten Ebern besucht wird: denn nie sind menschliche Füsse durch die dicken Wälder gedrungen. Aus dem Walde fiel ein Weg von dem Berge herunter, steil und gekrümmt und tief: doch war der Weg schön und anmuthig, denn an beiden Seiten waren überhangende bewachsene Felsen, und dann waren dunkle Hölen, aus denen Quellen hervorspritzten. .... Da kamen wir in das Thal von hohen Bergen umgränzt, deren schroffer Abhang mit Birken und Buchen und Eichen bedeckt war (15 ff.).

Am Abhange waren schrofe Abgründe und herüberhangende Felsen; doch waren die Felse und die Abgründe mit Buchen and Birken bewachsen, unter uns im unabsehlichen Thale standen hohe Eichen and Tannen, wie Buchwerk; eine reizende Scene! bey der die Seele in Entzückung zerschmilzt! Ungesättigt mit immer neuer Wollust irrt hier das Auge vom Thale auf den Berg, and vom Berge wieder ins Thal hin, und findet überall Ergötzen und Freude. Hier wollen wir uns lagern, rief Stephan, oft und lange ins tiefe unabsehliche Thal sehen. Nein, erwiederte Menalkas, hier wo der Weg sich dreht, ist die Aussicht noch schöner, denn hier erscheint auch jener Zug vom grünen Gebürge, das dort versteckt ist. Wir stritten uns so um den schönsten Gesichtspunkt (22).

Dicht am Fusse des Hügels lag im Schatten der Berge eine kleine, liebliche Stadt: so liegt im Schoosse der Mutter ein holdes schlafendes Kind. Hinter der Stadt war eine unabsehliche Landschaft, wie ein Garten, und nahe am Hügel waren grüne Thäler und abhangende Fluren, und hinter uns erhoben dunkel bewachsene Tannengebürge ihren Gipfel bis an die Wolken. Da wir auf einmal die paradiesische Abendsonne erblickten, blieben wir lange in stillem Entzücken da stehen, und weinten Freudenthränen (28).

Though it is difficult to tell whether this story exerted any influence on subsequent writers or not, yet, judged by its own merit, it is remarkable, because of the favorable mention of the primeval forest, overhanging rocks, and abysses, and the intense joy in nature for her own sake.[1]

With this possible exception (*Die Reise auf die Gebürge*), no work of German fiction before 1774 even approaches in sympathetic or effective treatment of nature Goethe's *Werther*. It might well be discussed at length, were it not familiar to every student of German literature. Laprade, and especially E. Schmidt and Biese, have analyzed with a masterly hand Werther's attitude toward nature, and have pointed out in detail the similarities and differences in Goethe's and Rousseau's treatment.[2] Sufficient is it then merely to sketch here briefly the use of nature as a dramatic background.

When Werther is first heard of it is May — in Germany the most charming month of the year. Hardly a day passes but he spends an hour in the open air, enjoying the cool shade of the tall trees.[3] When, a month later, he is about to meet Lotte for the first time, unpropitious clouds gather near the horizon and cause his companions to fear an approaching thunderstorm.[4] Just before Lotte discloses the identity of Albert, there is a change in the atmosphere, the lightning that has been hovering along the horizon grows more intense, and peals of thunder drown the strains of music.[5] Werther is told of Lotte's betrothal to Albert — the air clears, and a refreshing odor rises from the earth. The more Werther thinks, however, of his affection for Lotte, the less delight he takes in nature,[6] and when he looks out upon the snow-glittering fields over which a storm has just passed, he must needs think of himself and his wretched condition.[7] He begins to revel in the nature of Ossian, and roams about on sad and dreary November days, when those sick of love hunt for flowers.[8] As the last month of the year draws on, the time hostile to man, he loses all mastery over himself and seems to get relief only by hastening out into the awful December night; where he sees nature breaking her bonds, the rivers inundating all the country, and carrying destruction in their path.[9] Not much longer and he too will succumb to the violent tempest raging within him. In spite of rain and snow he climbs to the most dangerous precipice — but lives. Soon, however, the end draws near of him who is a son, a friend, a lover of nature.[10] He feels impelled, before leaving this world, to see for the last time

---

[1] The treatment of nature in other novels that appeared before *Werther* will be discussed at some future date.

[2] Cf. also Karl Hillebrand, Zeiten, Völker und Menschen, III, 331 ff.

[3] Der junge Goethe, III, 237.   [5] Ibid., 256.   [7] Ibid., 308.   [9] Ibid., 341.

[4] Ibid., 250.   [6] D. j. G., III, 293.   [8] Ibid., 335.   [10] Ibid., 365.

the fields, the woods, the skies — not bathed in sunshine, but in tears. He returns to his room, and, as he looks out of the window, the storm-laden clouds flit by — the storm in his breast has been allayed, his fate is sealed — calmness prevails. His favorite constellation, Charles's Wain, is still rising in the eternal sky — but he is gone.[1]

If Goethe had written nothing but *Werther*, he would still rank with the greatest of nature's interpreters. But add to this work his lyrics, and his pre-eminence as a poet of nature must be at once admitted. Such masterly interpretation of her manifold aspects, based on close observation of her phenomena, is not extant before his time. Two of her sublime elements, however, the ocean and the mountains, he reserved for later treatment.

[1] Ibid., 370.

III.

LETTERS.

THE eighteenth century has been properly called the "Age of Letter-Writing." The letter was the common form of expression; it recorded truthfully the inmost ideas and thoughts that stirred the people of the time. Hence it is one of the most important sources of information for the student of this century. The correspondence of the eighteenth century must be then considered, for in it nature will be found treated less conventionally than in the poetry of the time. It is true that in the collections of letters by various writers, edited in the eighteenth and nineteenth centuries, such as "Dreihundert Briefe aus zwei Jahrhunderten," "Briefe deutscher Gelehrten an den Herrn Geheimrath Klotz," "318 Briefe berühmter und geistreicher Männer und Frauen," there are no references whatever to nature. If, however, the letters of literary men and women be read, quite a different result will be arrived at. It will be seen presently that allusions to the world of nature increase about the middle of the century, and that close observation and genuine love of nature are distinctly traceable in the letters written shortly before the appearance of Werther.

On the threshold of the eighteenth century there is a letter writer whose letters mark, as Steinhausen[1] says, "eine neue Entwickelung im deutschen Briefe, welche ihren Höhepunkt in der zweiten Hälfte des Jahrhunderts hat." ELISABETH CHARLOTTE VON ORLEANS was the first since Luther to write letters in German "in der alten und volkstümlichen Art." Hence her volumes of letters must concern the present study, in that some stray but significant remarks regarding nature may be gleaned from them.

Comments on the weather are most frequent. Expressions like " das schönste," " das herrlichste wetter von der weldt,"[2] occur often. She dislikes, of course, rainy or stormy weather ("es regnete, alss wen mans mitt kübeln gösse,"[3] she says), and is always longing for spring[4] and summer; autumn, on the other hand, " hasse ich mehr als den winter," she writes.[5] She notes the signs of approaching spring:

---

[1] Geschichte d. d. Briefes, II, 110.   [3] June 28, 1721.

[2] Apr. 7, May 3, 1721.   [4] Mch. 22, 1721.   [5] Apr. 25, 1721.

"Alles ist grün im felt, die rossen undt grusselberg-hecken, das korn schiesst in ähren undt die gärtten seindt voller blumen, nartzissen undt jacinthen, margritten und noch andere blumger."[1] She enjoys the song of the nightingale,[2] and listens with as much pleasure to the frogs: "deren hore ich auch gantz chorus hir, die ich angenehmer findt, alss dass opera."[3]

The majesty of the ocean does not appeal to her, for she writes: "Ich finde das meer langweylig, verdriesslich undt unleydtlich."[4] Unlike Herder, as will be seen later, she fails to appreciate the delights of a voyage: "nichts alss lufft undt wasser zu sehen, dass ist mir gantz unleydtlich,"[5] but, strange to say, is fully conscious of the grandeur of thunder and lightning: "ich habe mich amussirt, ein zimblich lang donnerwetter zu sehen mit schönen wetterleuchten und blitzen; dass sehe ich recht gern."[6] Still more remarkable is her preference of the wild forest to the cultivated garden: "ich werde einen schönen gartten ehe müde, alss einen wilden waldt."[7] She foreshadows the fondness for idyllic life which became prevalent about the middle of the century, when she says: "aber offt in den strohütten leben die leutte mit grössern vergnügen, als in schöne palästen undt auff dem thron."[8]

The significance of Elisabeth Charlotte von Orleans in this study rests not so much on any artistic excellence of expression as on her preference of wild, free nature, her delight in some of the grand elements of nature (thunderstorms), and her early date. She has, however, also the negative importance of disliking other elements, such as the ocean.

The letters of Frau Gottsched form an interesting chapter in the correspondence of the eighteenth century. They refer chiefly to literary or personal matters, but occasionally give a glimpse of her view of nature. In reporting to her friend, Frau v. R., what she sees while traveling, she mentions some wonders of nature, and adds at once that the royal personages she has seen will certainly be of greater interest to her than these inanimate beauties.[9] At other times she complains of bad roads and disagreeable weather.[10] Quite in contrast with Klopstock, she dislikes winter sports, and speaks of them with contempt, while she is enjoying her warm room and her books: " Ich

---

[1] Mch. 16, 1719; Apr. 12, 1721, et passim.   [3] May 1, 1721.

[2] June 5, 1721.   [4] May 22, 1721.   [5] Ibid.

[6] May 23, 1722.   In another letter she calls it " ein magnific specktacle " (May 26, 1718).

[7] She wrote this from Versaille! (Sept. 21, 1710.)   [9] Cassel, July 20, 1753.

[8] Nov. 22, 1710.   [10] Sept. 6, 1749; Aug. 7, July 5, 1753.

sehe der Wuth dieser Menschen ganz gelassen aus meinem Fenster zu, setze mich an meinen Schreibtisch, und ergötze mich in meinem geheitzten Zimmer und mit meinen Büchern mehr als alle Schlitten-fahrer mit ihrer frostigen Lustbarkeit."[1] This utterance may well be taken as typical of her generation. She appreciates country life in accordance with the spirit of the time,[2] and expresses the opinion that only the peasant seems to enjoy to the fullest extent a sunrise or a sunset. The contemplation of a sunrise she would recommend to her friend as an effective means of curing hypochondria. In the same letter she mentions her intense interest in the starry heavens: " Das gestirnte Firmament hat in meiner ersten Jugend meine Neugier unzähligemal erreget. Mit welcher Aufmerksamkeit habe ich solches ganze Stunden lang betrachtet, mich dabey vergessen, aber meine Wissbegierde nie befriedigt."[3]

The letters of Frau Gottsched are typical of the second quarter of the century in that the emphasis is upon man rather than nature. She is aware, however, of the advantages of life in the country, for there one is in closer touch with nature than in the city.

The letters which E. v. KLEIST addressed to his friend Gleim con-tain some passages characteristic of his view of nature. The earliest reference is found in a letter dated March 9, 1746. He describes how in his dreams he walks with his friend along the seashore, listening to the murmuring of the blue waves, or on pleasant meadows, or in rustling bushes, where they can hear the goldfinch and the cuckoo. "Denn," he adds, "sehn wir die Sonne, die kurz zuvor gleich den Häuptern der Heiligen strahlte, sich hinter einem Walde in rosenfar-benen Wolken verbergen, wodurch die grünen Blätter der Wipfel das Ansehn gewinnen, als ob sie im Feuer glühten." Another time he describes rather picturesquely the arrival of spring: " Haben Sie heute den Frühling nicht vom Himmel gleiten gesehen? Ich sah ihn, er war aber ganz beschneit; er sah so weiss aus, wie ein Mädchen im Hemde."[4] He is so glad when spring comes that he hastens into the fields, unable to continue writing letters.[5] The month of November he dislikes, he says, as much as the Englishman does, except when Gleim calls on him.[6] He would like to write about winter, but cannot: "Mein Kopf is voller Winter-Bilder," he says; "aber kaum fange ich an zu arbeiten, so bin ich so echauffirt, dass ich es muss bleiben

---

[1] Jan. 10, 1735.
[2] July 18, 1752.
[3] Leipzig, Sept. 2, 1753.

[4] Mch. 21, 1747.
[5] Mch. 18, 1750.
[6] Oct. 20, 1751.

lassen."[1]   Once he complains of the bad weather in April, and another time mentions some beautiful days in March which have put him in good humor.[2]

In the letters of Kleist, the author of "Der Frühling," we are somewhat disappointed in the paucity of allusions to nature. His range is narrow; he entirely ignores the wild and terrible elements of nature.

There follow the letters of a man whose poems, as has been seen in another chapter, show the first distinct traces of the new feeling for nature.   It is therefore of more than usual interest to peruse his correspondence, and to ascertain whether the change of attitude is as noticeable in his letters as it was in his odes.

The year 1750 marks an important era in the life of KLOPSTOCK, for on the thirteenth of July of that year he left Quedlinburg in the company of Sulzer and Schuldheiss, and started on a trip to Switzerland, where he stayed about seven months.   During this period his works (cf. *Der Zürchersee* and *Friedensburg*) and letters show a more genuine and deeper love of nature than at almost any other time.   It cannot be said, however, that he went to Switzerland to see its beauties; they impressed themselves upon him while he was visiting his friends.

The homes of friends, as Klopstock himself says in a letter to Bodmer,[3] are more essential to a beautiful region than are mountains, valleys, and lakes.   So dear are his friends to him that he decides, just before beginning his Swiss tour, "unterwegs nur selten Thürme und Menschengesichte anzusehen, um recht sehr viel an seine Freunde zu denken."[4]   Apparently he does not keep his word, for the very first letters after his departure from his home mention the beautiful forests through which he and his friends pass.   "Von Arnstadt bis hierher [Rodach] haben wir lauter Tannen- und Fichtenwälder, die mit elysäischen Feldern untermischt waren, gesehn.   Vor Entzücken haben die Schweizer diese glückseligen Gegenden die Alpen genannt."[5]   And six days later he writes from Schaffhausen : "Der volle Mond begleitete uns die ganze Nacht durch die angenehmste waldige Gegend."

Klopstock and Schuldheiss speak of the beautiful regions between Ilmenau and Koburg, and call them "paradiesische Gegenden, die der Schweiz werth wären."[6]   After his arrival at Zürich, Klopstock writes :

---

[1] Dec. 18, 1753.   Three years later he writes: "Der Winter legt jetzt unserer Ehrbegierde, wie den Strömen und Bächen, den Zügel an" (Dec. 26, 1756).

[2] Apr., 1756; Mch., 1759.   [3] Nov. 28, 1749.   [4] July 12, 1750.   [5] July 13.   [6] Bamberg, July 16.

"Wenn ich an die kleinern Freuden, an die schönen Gegenden, an den vollen Genuss dieser schönen Gegenden . . . . denke . . . . wie sanft und mit wie vollem Herzen kann ich mich da dem Vergnügen ganz überlassen!"[1] The region about Winterthur surpasses in beauty all the landscapes he had seen up to that time.[2] Six years later, however, during his sojourn at Copenhagen, he experiences equal, if not greater, delight in the "Anhöhe von Mön die zum Malen schön und grösstenteils mit Waldungen bedeckt ist."[3]

If Klopstock had carried out his plan of ascending Mt. Rigi,[4] and had seen the sky below him, and had heard the thunder roll below him, as he indicates in his letter of the 25th of July, then, perhaps, he might have evinced more enthusiasm for the Alps than we can trace in his letters or works. In fact, in only one letter does he speak of the Alps—a letter, moreover, which was written before he had gotten into close proximity with the mountains. In the following words he describes the first sight of the "himmlischen Berge": "Eine Meile von hier, auf einem Gebirge, erblickten die Herren Schweizer ein paar Alpen. Sie wurden so entzückt, als wenn die Schiffer Land sehen. . . . ." Then he adds: "Es ist wahr, es war ein unvergleichlicher Anblick. Sie glänzten in der Ferne wie Silberwolken. . . . ."[5] He shows greater fervor when on the following day he sees the Falls of the Rhine: "Welch ein grosser Gedanke ist dieser Wasserfall!—Ich kann itzt davon weiter nichts sagen, ich muss diesen grossen Gedanken sehen und hören. . . . Hier im Angesichte des grossen Rheinfalls, in dem Getöse seines mächtigen Brausens, ... hier grüsse ich Euch, nahe und ferne Freunde! . . . . Hier möchte ich mein Leben zubringen und an dieser Stelle sterben, so schön ist sie."[6] Only one other outburst of this kind can be recorded during his Swiss sojourn. After a trip on Lake Zurich he writes to Schmidt:[7] "Ich kann Ihnen sagen, ich habe mich lange nicht so ununterbrochen, so wild, und so lange Zeit auf einmal, als diesen schönen Tag gefreut . . . . Wir stiegen unterwegs verschiedene Male aus, gingen an den Ufern spazieren, und genossen den schönsten Abend ganz!" Klopstock differs, it will be seen, from Rousseau in that he enjoys nature even when he is in the company of other human beings.

[1] July 25. Biese (313, note 4) must have overlooked these passages.
[2] Letter to Schmidt, Aug. 1 (or 15?).   [3] Sept. 4, 1756.
[4] Did he fail to carry it out because his friendship with Bodmer had been disrupted?   [5] July 20, 1750.
[6] Winter (27) says: "Diese Stelle bezeichnet den Höhepunkt seiner Empfindung."   [7] Aug. 1.

Six years after his journey to Switzerland he makes for the first time the acquaintance of the sea. But how meager are his comments on the ocean, when compared to those of Herder only thirteen years later! Yet he is in advance of the men of immediately preceding generations in that he not only enjoys his voyage, but is also aware, though on board a ship, of the grandeur of a storm at sea. He writes thus: "Als der Sturm kam, erschrak ich zwar anfangs ein wenig, fasste mich aber bald. . . . . Die See sah schön und schrecklich aus. Die Wellen gingen viel höher, schäumten viel mehr, und schlugen viel stärker an das Schiff, als vorher. . . . ."[1] This comment properly marks the transition attitude toward the ocean.

Klopstock enjoys country life, partly, however, because it is conducive to health.[2] Similarly he takes pleasure in skating,[3] as the following lines, directed to Gleim, show. The passage is of further interest, because it is one of the very few in which the poet evinces any humor. He says:[4] "Es ist doch ewig schade, liebster Gleim! dass Sie, wenn Sie kränkeln, sich nicht durch Schrittschuhlaufen kuriren können. Es ist eine von den besten Kuren: Recipe, Drei helle Stunden des Vormittags, Zwei des Nachmittags, Gute Gesellschaft! Viel Frühstück. Item ein wenig Nordwind zum Trunke bei der Arznei. Treib dieses acht Tage hinter einander! Probatum est!" Klopstock tried this prescription on himself, as he tells in a letter to Cäcilie Ambrosius, January 30, 1768. "Wie ich aber aufstand, da war so schön Wetter, und ich war so lange nicht auf dem Eise gewesen, und ich hatte auch die Bewegung wieder nöthig, dass ich statt zu schreiben, ausging, bis zu Tische auf dem Eise blieb, und nach Tische wieder ausging, und eben erst jetzt, es ist nach sechs Uhr, den schönen Mond, Orion und das Eis verlassen habe, nicht, dass ich nicht gern noch geblieben wäre, allein ich wollte Ihnen schreiben." He is so enthusiastic about skating, even when advanced in age, that he wants to make skaters of the "jüngsten und leichtesten Damen."[5]

Klopstock's correspondence is of the utmost importance in the history of the nature-sense. The terrible and grand in nature, mountains and ocean, are no longer ignored or disliked in these letters; a positive affection for them is expressed. Yet this is not the Rousseau feeling, which banished all thoughts of friends from one's mind when in communion with nature: Klopstock is in the company of his friends, or wishes that they were with him when he enjoys Alpine scenery, or gazes on the Falls of the Rhine.

[1] Sept. 4, 1756.   [3] Cf. his poems, chapter II, p. 47.
[2] Apr. 17, 1752, and Aug. 12, 1763.   [4] Mch. 1, 1766.   [5] Nov. 16, 1770.

The letters of SULZER, who accompanied Klopstock to Switzerland, deserve brief mention. Occasion will be taken to point out what place he occupies in the history of travels (cf. pp. 92, 96). It will be presently seen that his correspondence, so far at least as there has been opportunity to examine it, is also imbued with the modern spirit. In his earlier letters spring is frequently mentioned. He writes to Gleim, for instance: " Ein schöner Frühling-Morgen (ich steh' um 6 Uhr auf) hat alles in mir rege gemacht. . . . ." And, in continuing, says of the beauties of nature: "die Natur hat unendliche Schönheiten, die man nicht erschöpfen wird, wenn auch alle die elenden Scribenten die besten Poeten würden."[1] Three years later, when longing for the first signs of spring, he communicates this rather humorous suggestion: "Ich wollte, dass dem Winter ein Stein an den Hals gehängt, und dass er in's Meer versenkt würde."[2] And yet he suggests to Sam. Gotthold Lange to write a poem in praise of winter.[3]

When, in 1750, he starts on his journey to Switzerland in the company of Klopstock and Schuldheiss, he complains at first of bad roads,[4] but becomes oblivious to the discomforts of traveling when he reaches mountains and valleys. He gives a detailed account of his experiences, of the many dangerous places through which he passes, rushing waters and narrow paths along precipices, and then closes the report in these words: "Alles Fürchterliche aber ward von uns kaum bemerkt; die Schönheit der Gegend setzte uns in den höchsten Grad des Vergnügens."[5]

It is interesting to note that later in life his attitude toward nature had changed, as he tells in a letter from Nice.[6] In his youth the landscape about that city would have satisfied all his desires; " aber bei meinem herannahenden Alter," he says, "hat die Natur mit allen ihren Schönheiten nicht Kraft genug, mich ganz zufrieden zu stellen."

Barring a stray reference or two in regard to the beauty of Alpine scenery, Klopstock and Sulzer stand alone, for a time at least, in their attitude toward nature.[7] In the letters of Rabener and Liscow no allusions whatever to nature are found, in those of Gessner[8] and Gellert but few and rather insignificant ones. The correspondence of the last-named will be briefly discussed.

[1] Mch. 20, 1745.   [2] Mch. 30, 1748.   [3] Dec. 26, 1746.   [4] July 13.   [5] July 15   [6] Dec. 11, 1775.

[7] Cf. Waser's letter, Zurich, June 10, 1746: " Es ist ein herrliches Spectacul die schweizerischen Gebirge anzusehen . . . . ," and Hagedorn's letter (1750), in which he expresses the desire to spend spring and summer in Switzerland " in den malerischen Gegenden, zwischen hohen Bäumen und Bergen . . . ." (Stäudlin's Collection).

[8] His letter to Fuesslin is interesting because of his characterization of Claude Lorraine (anmutig), S. Rosa (melancholisch, wild), and Poussin (edel und gross).

" Habe Auge und Ohr für die Schönheiten der Natur, und lerne Dich ihrer erfreuen, so oft Du sie empfindest," says GELLERT, in " Lehren eines Vaters für seinen Sohn." But he himself only rarely followed this advice, if one may judge from his works, letters, and diary. When he does mention nature, which happens in a few places,[1] he speaks of it either from the pietistic or the utilitarian point of view, as is shown in some of his poems ("Die Himmel rühmen des Ewigen Ehre"), and in the seventeenth chapter of his "Moralische Vorlesungen," which contains this brief but characteristic comment on mountains : "Die Berge sind wesentliche Schönheiten der Natur, wenn wir ihre verschiedene Betrachtungen betrachten, Dünste zu sammeln, Metalle zu zeugen, ... die Aussicht angenehm zu machen. . . . . Wozu Berge mit ewigem Schnee und Eise bedeckt ?" he asks, and answers at once : "Zum Nutzen und Vergnügen des Ganzen ! "

Gellert's letters and diary (of the year 1761) are further evidence of his lack of nature-sense. Owing to the continued illness, which is frequently mentioned in his correspondence, the country has as little charm for him as the city.[2] Thus he writes to Fräulein von Schön-feld[3] : "Ich sehe die Baumblüthe vor mir, und sie lacht mich nicht an. Ich höre die Nachtigallen und bleibe immer kaltsinnig. Ich gehe nach Meineweh in das Fasanenholz, und es ist, als ob mir jeder Baum etwas vorzuwerfen hätte." Once he speaks of the beautiful meadows and clover in spring,[4] and several times of the weather, especially when it is disagreeable.[5] His travels (to Berlin, Dresden, Carlsbad) are a source of annoyance to him,[6] and hence he fails to appreciate whatever natural scenery there may be along the way.

In rather marked contrast to the letters of Gellert are those of his correspondent, Demoiselle Lucius. She describes a moonlight walk and all that she observed the while in the following words : " Wir gingen von acht bis zehn Uhr im grossen Garten, im Mondlichte, in der sanftesten Luft, unter dem abwechselndesten Himmel, und in einer so ruhigen Stille — man hörte nichts als den einförmigen Gesang des Grashüpfers und einzelne vorübergehende Spazierende. Es war ausserordentlich schön."[7] Another time she tells him how deeply nature affected her: "Wir setzten uns an einen erhabnen Ort, von welchem wir die Landschaft umher übersahen. Es war ausserordentlich schön, die Luft so sanft schmeichelnd, der Himmel bedeckt und

---

[1] Because his works contain but few references to nature, it seemed preferable to insert them here rather than in the preceding chapter.

[2] Apr. 13, Sept. 4, 1760.   [4] May 22, 1759.   [6] Mch. 2, Apr. 19, 1752.

[3] Bonau, May 20, 1760.   [5] Mch. 27, 1756; Oct. 3, 1758, et passim.   [7] Aug. 18, 1767.

doch nicht trübe, das lachendste Grün über die Felder gebreitet . . . .
der frohe Gesang der Lerche und auf der andern Seite das Geschwätz
der mancherley Vögel in dem jungen Laube der Bäume des Gartens
und ausser diesem die ruhigste Stille, ganz feyerlich bis zur ange-
nehmsten Melancholie und doch nicht zu ernsthaft oder traurig. . . . .
Alles rührte mich angenehm und ich hatte eine der glücklichsten
Stunden."[1]

We have quoted at length from her letters to show that the nature-
sense was rapidly growing delicate even with those who have left no
traces in literature.

Before turning to the letters of Herder and Goethe, brief note may
be made of those that were written by the Anacreontic poets. Like
their works, these letters show few, if any, traces of the new attitude
toward nature that was seen breaking forth in the odes and letters of
Klopstock. Friendship is their chief topic, and nature serves only
occasionally as a background for it. One might expect to find, as is
really the case, that most frequent mention is made of beautiful spring
and dreary winter. There are — it may be said at once — more references to the world of nature in the letters of Gleim, Jacobi, and
Wieland than in those of the other poets belonging to the group
under consideration.

To begin with GLEIM: He sees the shortcomings of country
life which are due to the lack of intercourse with many citizens,[2] and
goes to the country because of the "schöne Frühlingswetter und eine
kleine Brunette."[3] When he contemplates a trip to the "schönen
Gegenden auf dem Harz,"[4] or to other parts in Germany, he does it
chiefly in the hope of traveling with friends, enjoying their company,
and meeting or making the acquaintance of other people. He is
interested in the "fürtreflichen Gegenden" of the Hartz mountains,
through which he wanders with his friend Klopstock, but would probably enjoy them much more, if "sein Uz" were there, too.[5]

In the letters of J. G. JACOBI the emphasis is also upon man rather
than nature. The walks, the garden, the mountain, are of interest to
him, because Gleim had been there.[6] He visits the latter in spite of
cold nights and stormy days.[7] He cannot bear the heavy, melancholy
fog, through which he had to pass on his way to Kennern; but, as he

---

[1] Berggiesshübel, Apr. 17, 1769.   [2] Sept. 7, 1741.   [3] June, 1742.   [4] July 8, 1753.

[5] Sept. 24, 1762. Similarly he would be pleased with the flowers in his garden, were his friend Jacobi
with him and singing about them. (Letter to Jacobi, Halberstadt, Oct. 1, 1767.)

[6] May 16, Aug. 24, 1767.   [7] Nov. 25, Dec. 2, 1767.

says :[1] "Hätt' [der Winter] blos seinen unförmlichen Bart geschüttelt, und meinen Wagen voll geschneyt; dann wär' er immer von mir ausgelacht worden." As he drives over the frozen river Saale, and sees on both sides large blocks of ice marking the road, he says : "der Anblick war ganz poetisch." He likes winter better than autumn, and to show what little influence nature has upon him he decides to sing in his room of the "schönsten Jahreszeiten, den [Herbst] Stürmen zum Trotz."—One other passage found in a letter to Klotz should be mentioned here. Jacobi is in search of a melancholy spot and thinks of the Rabeninsel, "wo ich von dem dichten Gehölze und von dem Gekrächze schwarzer Vögel mir vieles versprach," but before long considers the ruins of Giebichenstein superior. "Eingefallene Thürme, Felsen und Felsenklüfte: O wie schön lässt es sich da klagen !"

At the age of eighteen WIELAND writes to Bodmer :[2] "Ich liebte die Einsamkeit sehr [im vierzehnten Jahre], und brachte oft ganze Tage und Sommernächte im Garten zu, die Schönheiten der Natur zu empfinden und abzuschildern." This remark would lead one to expect a strong appreciation of nature in Wieland, the man. It is with disappointment, however, that one reads his correspondence during the sojourn in Switzerland from 1752 to 1760. Instead of letters full of allusions to the natural scenery round about him, only one or two stray remarks in them indicate that Swiss landscapes made some impression upon him. After leaving Zurich he misses in Bern the charming location and environment of the former town, and is convinced "dass die Schönheit der Häuser und Strassen in Bern kein Ersatz [ist] für die angenehmen Promenaden und den See zu Zürich."[3] It is no surprise, then, not to find a word in his letters anent the country through which he passes on his way to Ilmenau (1769), to Coblentz (1771), and again to Zurich (1796).[4]

Characteristic of his feeling for nature are these lines, addressed to his friend Riedel :[5] "Ich wohne im Gartenhaus nahe der Stadt . . . . wo ich die angenehmste Landaussicht von der Welt habe. . . . . Hier sehe ich die Knaben baden ; ich rieche den lieblich erfrischenden Geruch des Heues ; ich sehe . . . . ein langes angenehmes Thal . . . . und über demselben eine Reihe ferner blauer Berge . . . . und mit diesem Prospekt vor mir, sitze ich und — reime."

His strong dislike for winter and stormy weather, and his longing

---

[1] Jan. 17, 1768.   [2] Tübingen, Mch. 6, 1752.   [3] Bern, July 4, 1759.   [5] Biberach, Aug. 24, 1768.

[4] Except this comment in a letter to Frau Herder (July 3): "herrlich schöne Natur die uns umgibt . . . . himmlische Sommertage."

for, and delight in, spring he expresses time and again, thus showing his kinship with the Anacreontic poets and with their attitude toward nature. Illustrative of many such remarks are the following:[1] "Schon der 27. April und kein Anschein von Frühling; nicht einmal eine arme Schwalbe, die uns Hoffnung machte, dass er kommen werde. Ich lebe nur noch an einem Faden, so massleidig macht mich diese verwünschte 'décrépitude de la nature.'" More forcibly he expresses himself to Merck:[2] "Es ist mir aber in diesen vergangenen Wochen wegen des stürmischen schlechten Wetters . . . . meistens so dumm, schnuppicht und schlappicht zu Muth gewesen, dass es mir ohnmöglich war, etwas anders als einen Frachtzettel zu schreiben." In another letter he speaks of the "kalten windigen dreckfarbigen Tagen" and the "abscheulich raschen Übergänge von Wärme und Kälte und die rauhen flegelhaften Winde aus Norden und über dem Thüringer Wald her."[3] In spring, on the other hand, his joy knows no bounds. "Die ganze Natur fängt jetzt an zu leben und zu weben, zu grünen und zu blühen," he writes to Gleim, May 1, 1775. "Mit jedem Tage schiesst der Lebensstrom stärker durch Ihre Adern." Three years later he reports to Merck his observations in his garden, and the intense joy he derives from watching the growth and development of plant and animal, and adds: "Ich athme die milde, lieblich scharfe herzausdehnende Luft, und sauge die Strahlen der herzerquickenden Sonne nicht um des Reims willen, sondern in vollem Ernst mit Wonne ein. . . . ." He closes by saying: "Da alles um mich her knospet und schwillt und plazt und grünet und zu blühen beginnt, werdet Ihr leicht denken dass ich nicht allein zurückbleiben werde."[4] One other quotation should find a place here, so that it may be seen he was not a total stranger to the new feeling for nature. In 1775 he writes:[5] "[Wir] hatten . . . . das prächtigste Gewitter, das ich je erlebt habe . . . . Ich weiss nichts Rührenderes als solche Scenen."

As in the works of Wieland, so in his letters, one can trace a faint but genuine feeling for nature.

While the letters of Klopstock show, as has been seen, the first distinct traces of the new feeling for nature, those of HERDER are already thoroughly modern in spirit. Particularly is this true of the letters that were written in the years intervening between his sojourn at Riga and his removal to Weimar (1764–75).

But even when a boy, Herder found recreation and pleasure in frequenting those outdoor spots where he could read undisturbed in the

[1] Apr. 27, 1771.   [2] May 5, 1779.   [3] June 1, 1778.   [4] Apr. 12, 1778.   [5] June 19.

midst of blossoms and singing of birds, and at other times enjoyed his
favorite walk along the Mohrunger-See and through the "Paradieses-
Wäldchen."[1]   Later in life he perused, in similar surroundings, Diderot
and Gessner and "Felix Hess,"[2] and took delight in sauntering through
wood and dale,[3] especially at an early morning hour.   "Die Leute
halten mich für einen grossen Gelehrten," he writes to his bride, "weil
ich mich Morgens 4 Uhr in den Wäldern umhertreibe."[4]

Of his sojourn at Riga there are but few reminiscences.   In a letter
to Merck he recalls the approach of winter in Livonia.   He writes:[5]
"Ich habe Ihren letzten Brief mit dem traurigen Schauder gelesen,
mit dem ich in Liefland mehr als Einmal das Hinanwehen des Winter-
frostes gefeiert!   Ein unnennbares Rauschen ging durch die Luft!
die Zweige des Baums bebten, das grüne Blättchen krümmte sich voll
Angst zusammen, und in wenigen Tagen lags gelb zur Erde.   Meine
Seele hat diese Krümmung der Seele bei Ihnen sehr gefühlet."   He
loved to live by the sea, and during his residence in Bückeburg, and
in the early years at Weimar, ardently wished for a call to Kiel, or to
that region, for, as the "Erinnerungen" (I, 149) say, "das Wohnen
an der See hatte für ihn einen grossen Reiz, der ihm von Riga her
unauslöschlich geblieben war."

The spring of 1769 marks an important turning-point in Herder's
career: he made the well-known voyage from Riga to Nantes, the fruit
of which was the "Reisejournal"— a document which, according to
Koch,[6] "lässt die ganze gährende Kraft der nach freier Umgestaltung
von Litteratur und Leben ringenden Jugend erkennen."   In the history of the nature-sense it is, however, not quite so important.   If one
take away the few data pertaining to his surroundings, not much that
is essential to the understanding of his line of thought will be lost.
And yet, as Haym says,[7] "ohne den vorgegangenen Scenenwechsel
wäre dieser Monolog niemals gehalten, wäre er jedenfalls so nicht
gehalten worden."   Of Herder, during this trip, the "Erinnerungen"
(I, 120) give us a rather full description, consisting largely of his own
utterances.   "Er war beständig auf dem Verdeck in freier Luft. . . . .
Mehrmals sagte er uns: nie habe er sich gesunder gefühlt als auf dem

---

[1] Erinnerungen, I, 10.   [3] To Hamann, Riga, Mch., 1769.

[2] Letter to Caroline Flachsland, Oct. 24, 1772, and to Lavater, June, 1774.—Whenever he received
a letter from Hamann, "dann musste er hinaus ins Freie, seine ganze Seele war bewegt" (Erinnerungen,
I, 65).   No wonder he complains to Merck about Strassburg (Sept., 1770): "Hier ist einmal kein
Wald, kein Ort, wo man mit seinem Buche und Genius einmal im Schatten liege."

[4] Erinnerungen, I, 206.   [6] Gesch. d. d. Lit., 176 (Sammlung Göschen).

[5] Bückeburg, Sept., 1771.   [7] Herder nach seinem Leben u. seinen Werken dargestellt, I, 318.

Meer; der immerwährende Genuss der freien Luft, die grossen Gegenstände von Meer und Himmel, Aufgang und Untergang der Sonne (so
einzig auf der See!), die Nächte, die electrisch funkelnden Meeres-
wellen, der Sternenhimmel, der Mond, Regen, Ungewitter—alles dies
wirkte gross und mächtig auf seine stark und innig fühlende, empfin-
dungsvolle, phantasiereiche Seele." [1] In Herder's letters but few references to this voyage are found. As he passes the island of Moen,
which, as Klopstock thought, " zum Malen schön," he writes to Hart-
knoch: [2] " Schöne Abende und Tage, und oft eine spiegelglatte helle
See. . . . . Es fehlt also zu meiner Reise nicht als scherzende Del-
phinen und Meerpferd' unter ihnen." [3] To his friend Hamann he
confesses the inestimable benefit derived from being on a ship for six
continuous weeks : " Ich stürzte mich aufs Schiffe ohne Musen, Bücher [4]
und Gedanken . . . . und habe also die ganze 6 Wochen . . . . nichts
anders können als träumen—blos sich, dem Himmel und dem Meer
übergeben—o Freund, da lehren uns Träume von 6 Wochen mehr, als
Jahre von Bücherreflexionen." [5] Similarly, the following passage from
the " Reisejournal," which one is tempted to quote at length : " Was
giebt ein Schiff, das zwischen Himmel und Meer schwebt, nicht für
weite Sphäre zu denken! Alles gibt hier dem Gedanken Flügel und
Bewegung und weiten Luftkreis! Das flatternde Segel, das immer
wankende Schiff, der rauschende Wellenstrom, die fliegende Wolke,
der weite unendliche Luftkreis!" " So ward ich Philosoph auf dem
Schiffe—Philosoph aber, der es noch schlecht gelernt hatte, ohne Bücher
und Instrumente aus der Natur zu philosophiren. Hätte ich dies
gekonnt, welcher Standpunkt, unter einem Mast auf dem weiten Ocean
sitzend über Himmel, Sonne, Sterne, Mond, Luft, Wind, Meer, Regen,
Seegrund philosophiren." Then, as he looks upon the water, he comments on his favorite comparison of water to air: " Wie sich Welle in
Welle bricht : so fliessen die Luftundulationen und Schälle ineinander.
. . . . Wie die Welle das Schiff umschliesst : so die Luft den sich
bewegenden Erdball." [6] " Wasser ist eine schwerere Luft : Wellen und
Ströme sind seine Winde : die Fische seine Bewohner : der Wasser-
grund ist eine neue Erde." When comparison is made with the letters
of the first quarter of the century in which the ocean is mentioned, say

---

[1] Reminiscences of these impressions we note during his Italian journey, in " Kalligone," III : 23,
and in the " Unterhaltungen u. Briefe über die ältesten Urkunden." See p. 50.

[2] Erinnerungen, I, 134.   [4] He read Ossian, however. Cf. *Briefwechsel über Ossian.*

[3] Cf. also " Reisejournal " : " Ich erinnere mich noch der himmlischen Nächte, die ich vor Koppen-
hagen hatte."

[5] Nantes, 1769 (?).   [6] See also *Älteste Urkunde*, Pt. I, 5.

those of Charlotte of Orleans, one can realize the change of attitude toward nature which has taken place in Germany in the course of fifty years. Herder is the precursor of this new feeling for the grandeur and sublimity of the ocean, but had ere long followers in such men as Stolberg [1] and Lichtenberg. [2]

During his residence at Bückeburg, however, Herder lived in closer communion with nature than at any previous time. The following facts may account for it : first, he was dissatisfied in both his official and social life; [3] secondly, thoughts of love were uppermost in his mind : he was writing almost daily to his bride-elect, Caroline Flachsland; and, thirdly, he was attracted by the charm and beauty of the surrounding country. He communicates to Caroline the joy he derives from the romantic country in which he lives; [4] "Eben das Feld, wo Hermann focht und Varus geschlagen ward; noch jetzt ein fürchterliches, kühnes romantisches Thal, mit sonderbaren Gebirgen umgeben." In Pyrmont he sees "die grosse, schöne, heilsame Natur" and "ein eignes, halb düsteres und eingeschlossenes Thal," and adds : "Ist diese Welt nicht schön ? Wie dumme Leute gibt es, die nichts von ihr fühlen — Feldthiere und Koththiere!" [5] He is infatuated with his home and its environment. He lives in seclusion, in the midst of nature, mountain, and forest, filled with the songs of nightingales round about him. "Die Blumen und Knospen brechen jetzt aus der Erde! da liege ich bis in die Nacht!" he exclaims. [6]

Almost every letter exchanged by the two lovers contains some allusion to nature. They tell each other of their delightful walks in forests and in the country, the romantic spots where they would lie musing for hours, [7] sometimes even after nightfall, [8] and the beautiful autumn days with their mists. [9] Caroline, especially, is fond of autumn, whereas Herder rejoices much more at the return of spring. He is enraptured with the "romantische Feen-Johanniszeit der Bohnenblüthe und Johanniswürmchen und des Aehrenkorns, der Rose und der Nachtigall," and says of this songster : "Sie schlägt mir vor dem Fenster bis ins Bett — und so tief aus der Brust, und so tief in die Brust hinein!" [10]

[1] See p. 86.

[2] Cf. letter to Pastor Amelung, June 21, 1786.

[3] Haym, I, 471.

[4] Erinnerungen, I, 221.

[5] July, 1772.

[6] May 11, 1771.

[7] Caroline to Herder, May 6, June 14, Nov., 1771; April, May 8, 25, June, 1772.

[8] See Herder's letter (after) June 15, 1771, and Caroline's (beginning of) July, 1772.

[9] Darmstadt, Oct., 1771.

[10] May, 1772; Apr. 19, 1772; Apr. 10, 1773, et passim; and Caroline's letters, Oct. 9, Dec. 12, 1772, etc.

Of still greater interest, however, are the reports that the two lovers send each other, after they have witnessed a sunset, a sunrise, or a moonlight scene. Herder's letter to Caroline dated September, 1771,[1] is most valuable for our present purpose, and may therefore bear quoting at length. He writes : "Wir ritten voll Gedanken zurück : es war Abend : die Sonne ging unter, und der Mond ging auf, der schönste Mond, den ich gesehn. Empfindungen voll Schmerz und bittrer Wehmuth gaben im Mondenschein den schönsten Gegenden, voll Höhen und Thal und Wald und Wiesen, eine romantische Anmuth, als wir uns gemeiniglich im Elysium träumen! Allemal, wenn wir auf einer steilen Höhe hinauf, oder einen finstern Wald . . . . durch waren, und sich dann mit Einemmal eine Mondgegend, ein weites Strahlenthal eröffnete, das in Dämmerung floss, war ich Allemal in einer neuen Welt und so sprachlos und traumversenkt kamen wir endlich ins Nachtquartier. . . . ." The following morning he records these impressions : "Vor Sonnenaufgang in der frühesten Dämmerung zu Pferde, sahen wir die Morgenröthe mit jedem werdenden neuen Strahle, mit jeder neuen Veränderung des Himmels und der ganzen Welt! Die ganze Welt war ein stiller, feierlicher, sanfter Tempel Gottes, wo ich versunken war, und nichts denken konnte, als dass auch in solchem ewigen Ton der Morgenröthe der Tempel meiner Seele wäre — und die Sonne ging auf! Je höher sie trat, desto mehr war Alles lauter, erleuchteter, einförmiger ; die Schönheit der Natur nahm ab, und ward Glanz, blosse Pracht — ists nicht beinahe so mit allem Glück — es ist am Schönsten im Anbruch, in der Morgenröthe . . . ." At another time he describes what he sees while walking in the twilight of an autumn day: "Stellen Sie sich auf der einen Seite eine Kette kleiner Gebirge voll Wald vor . . . . die nun in dem seidnen Nebel des Herbstes und der Abendsonne flossen : davor Wiesen und Gärten ; auf der andern Seite das ritterliche gräfliche Schloss, das sich im hellen stillen Wasser spiegelt : die Abendsonne vor mir ; . . . . ich warf mich unweit einiger Kuppeln romantischer schwarzer Bäume auf einen wilden Hügel, an einen Wasserfall, der mit doppeltem Guss schneller und langsamer, dunkler und heller, fiel. Um ihn viel wildes Weidengebüsche, um mich alle wilden Blumen, die in Shakspears Feen- und Liebesliedern vorkommen — Berge, Sonne, Abend um mich ! "

On the whole, Herder represents the new spirit more fully than any of the other letter-writers mentioned thus far. He notes the permanent and the evanescent in nature. He observes with a keen eye

---

[1] Erinnerungen, I, 211.

the natural scenery about him, and feels that there are bonds of sympathy between himself and nature; he is, moreover, the first to give expression to the feeling that the ocean can afford us an adequate conception of grandeur and sublimity.

A contemporary of Herder, and in some respects resembling him in his view of nature, was the physicist LICHTENBERG.

His letters must be considered, if one wishes fully to understand his nature-sense, for his works give but a slight indication of it, after it has been once traced in his correspondence. Since the quotations in these works are few in number, it may not be amiss to introduce them here instead of in Chapter II. They are as follows: " Der Herbst zählt der Erde die Blätter wieder zu, die sie dem Sommer geliehn hat." " Der Gang der Jahreszeiten ist ein Uhrwerk, wo ein Guckguck ruft, wenn es Frühling ist." Of particular significance is the following, because it is indicative of the new attitude : " Grosse Dinge gesehen zu haben, z. B. einen grossen Sturm, muss unstreitig dem ganzen Gehirn eine andere Stimmung geben, und man kann sich daher nicht genug in solche Lagen bringen."[1]

The close sympathy between himself and nature Lichtenberg describes rather fully in a letter to Madame Dietrich.[2] Because it is so thoroughly modern in spirit, it may well bear lengthy quotation. " Sie können nicht glauben," he begins, "was für ein Abend es gewesen ist. Die Luft, die den ganzen Tag über beinahe in einem kochenden Zustande gewesen war, fing nun an, in dem entzückendsten Gleichgewicht zwischen Wärme und Kühlung, welches allein schon in allem Fleisch die schönsten Empfindungen hervorbringen kann, stille zu stehen. Von dem angenehmen Wasser bei meinem Garten wurde ein so feiner Himmel zurückgeworfen, als man nur immer zu Darmstadt sieht. Einige Schwäne, die einen feinen Abend eben so gut zu schmecken wissen . . . . plätscherten in dem Wiederschein des Himmels. . . . . Anfangs fuhr noch dann und wann ein kleines Wünschchen durch meinen Kopf, das mich etwas beunruhigte, bis es endlich ebenfalls in mir zu einem Gleichgewicht kam, zu welchem mich die Natur einzuladen schien, und welches ich für einen so reizenden Zustand erkenne."

In 1773 Lichtenberg went to Heligoland. He is one of the first to call attention to the beauty of the island, and, because he was a scientist, he observed also the physical condition of the country. He recorded, furthermore, some of the phenomena of the sea which were

[1] Verm. Schriften, II, 105, 108, 136.   [2] Hannover, June 26, 1772.

noted about the same time by Forster in his travels; such as the phosphorescence of the sea.[1] Twenty years later he is still full of admiration for this same island and expresses his feelings thus: "Wer so etwas noch nicht gesehen hat, datirt ein neues Leben von einem solchen Anblick. . . . . Ich glaube jeder Mann von Gefühl, der das Vermögen hat, sich diesen grossen Genuss zu verschaffen, und es nicht thut, ist sich Verantwortung schuldig. Nie habe ich mit so vieler, fast schmerzhafter Theilnehmung an meine hinterlassenen Freunde in den dumpfigen Städten zurückgedacht, als auf Helgoland. Ich weiss nichts hinzuzusetzen, als: man komme und sehe und höre."[2] On his voyage he did not fail to observe the northern lights, and what is known as the "Kälbertanz" he describes in these words: "Man kann sich nichts fürchterlicher vorstellen. Die Wellen, die an die verborg-nenen Klippen und Sände anstossen, steigen in allerlei Richtungen als ein weisser Schaum in die Höhe, welches in einiger Entfernung aussieht, als wenn eine Heerde weisser Kühe sehr muthwillig durch einander sprängen."[3]

Lichtenberg's letters are further evidence of the spread of the new feeling at the end of the third quarter of the century. They show that he not only observes closely, but that he has an eye for the beauties of nature as well. He deserves credit for spreading the knowledge of beautiful regions hitherto unknown.

Of the men that were more or less closely connected with the "Göttinger Hain," the most important from the present point of view are Bürger, Hölty, and Friedrich Stolberg. Their letters, so far as they are of concern here, show that at the end of the third quarter of the century a genuine love of nature was no longer very unusual.

In BÜRGER's letters (i. e., those written before 1775) only spring and the coming of it are spoken of occasionally. These references are found chiefly in his letters to Boie; they call attention to the depend-ence of the poet's mood on the "goings-on" in nature. In May he writes with enthusiasm of the "paradiesischen Lenz": "Er entzückt und begeistert mich so sehr, dass ich kein Wort singen und sagen kann."[4] And again, one year later: "Der schönste Frühling um mich her fängt an, meine Lebens Geister aufzukochen. Noch ist alles blosser Dunst; ich bin aber neugierig welch ein schnurriges fixum an der Retorte hangen bleiben wird."[5]

HÖLTY is much more a poet of nature than is Bürger, and his

---

[1] Stade, June 19, 1773. [3] July 26, 1773. [4] May 17, 1773. [5] Niedeck, May 12, 1774.
[2] *Warum hat Deutschland noch kein grosses öffentliches Seebad?*

letters bear out this fact.   He says in a letter to Voss[1] that only in the country has he any desire to write poems, and only there can he live ideally.   "Wenn ich an das Land denke, so klopft mir das Herz. Eine Hütte, ein Wald daran, eine Wiese mit einer Silberquelle und ein Weib in meiner Hütte, ist alles was ich auf diesem Erdboden wünsche." Spring, especially, he wishes to enjoy in the country;[2] if he were to stay in the city, "dann würde er verschimmeln."[3]   When he is in the country, then, he writes, "bekommt mein Geist einen ganz andern Schwung.   Ich höre noch die letzten sterbenden Schläge der Nachtigall; ich sitze unter einem vom schönen blauen Himmel durchschimmerten Baume im Grase, oder wandle einsam im Walde herum."[4]   And in autumn, when the meadows are fragrant with the odor of hay, he lies at twilight in the hayloft and, as he says, "hänge meinen Phantasieen nach, bis der silberne Mond am Himmel hervorgeht, und mich angenehm überrascht."[5]

FRIEDRICH STOLBERG is even more interesting than the melancholy Hölty, but of less concern to this study, because many of his letters were written after the time-limit set therein.   He plays, however, so important a rôle in the history of the nature-sense that he may not be altogether omitted.   His letters, like those of Herder, are of particular value because of their allusions to the ocean.

The ocean was familiar to him from his childhood.   The Stolberg family was wont to spend the winter in Copenhagen, the summer in Rondstedt, "in den schönsten und freundlichsten Gegenden Seelands unfern des Meergestades."[6]   The beauties of nature with which Friedrich became acquainted here filled him with enthusiasm.   "Keinen Ort habe ich so geliebt als Rondstedt," he writes to his sister Catherine,"[7] "die freundlichen Buchenhaine . . . . das erhabene Meer, das bald roth von der auf- oder untergehenden Sonne lächelt und bald mit allen Schrecken Gottes sich rüstet."[8]   This ocean he missed in Switzerland (1775), and again in Eutin.[9]   From this city he writes very interestingly regarding the symphony of nature and the ocean:[10]   "Ich habe einen Freund, der, wenn er traurig ist, gleich an's Clavier geht und spielt.   Aber die vollbesaitete und vollstimmige Symphonie der Natur — was sind gegen die alle Claviere?   Und wahrlich, das Meer ist eines ihrer grossen Instrumente, scheint mir nicht Saite, sondern Stimme, so belebt ist es."   Klopstock, it seems to him, resembles the

[1] April, 1774.   [3] May 14, 1776.   [5] Aug. 21, 1775.   [7] Aug. 24, 1775.

[2] Zelle, Oct. 10, 1775.   [4] July 18, 1776.   [6] Janssen, I, 5.   [9] April 16, 1779.

[8] See also letter to his brother Christian, Oct. 24, 1780.   [10] Oct. 14, 1779.

sea. "Der Ocean, der mehr als irgend einer fluthen und ebben kann, den die stärksten Stürme empört und Blitze durch die geöffneten Wogen bis zum tiefsten Grund erleuchtet haben, wie ist er so still, so sonnenerhelt!"[1] Utterances like those just quoted prove beyond the shadow of a doubt that Stolberg's apostrophes to the ocean did not take rise in his imagination, but were the true product of his experience.

It has been observed in another chapter that his sojourn at Göttingen gave rise to several poems. He thinks that he never saw so beautiful a country as that about Ilsenburg. He likes to watch the Ilse as it flows from one rocky cascade to another.[2] Like Rousseau, he is fond of nature untouched by human hand,[3] as he finds it, for instance, in the primeval forest. The trees that were uprooted by the storm seem to him picturesque, and one mighty oak which was dead, with the exception of one living and leafy branch, attracts his attention. Whereupon he remarks: "Es ist doch so schön und interessant zu sehen, wie Mama Natur sich amüsirt, wenn sie allein ist."[4]

His Swiss tour furnished the themes for the poems *An die Natur*, *Der Felsenstrom*, and others. The first was inspired by the Falls of the Rhine. This phenomenon would naturally appeal to a "Stürmer und Dränger," and Stolberg was not the man to be left unaffected at the sight of it. He fairly bubbles over with an enthusiasm almost as great as Heinse's, when, a few years later, he reaches the Falls. "Es riss mich hin," writes Stolberg, "wie mich nie etwas hingerissen hat. Stelle Dir den schnellen, reissenden Rheinstrom vor, wie er von Felsenufern gedrängt wird, wie sich hohe, hohe Felsen in seinen Lauf stellen, wie er an sie himmelhoch schäumt, sich über sie hinweg reisst und sich vierzig Ellen tief in's Thal stürzt. . . . . Mit der Schnelle des Blitzes braust der Strom hernieder, so schnell, dass mir dabei oft schwindlig ward."[5] No wonder he is filled with wrath when Campe compares "die unnütze Bewegung des Stromes mit den Luftsprüngen unserer Kraftgenies."[6] Stolberg visited the Falls no less than three times, and each time he was filled with astonishment. He expresses himself thus: "Grauenvolles, doch seliges Staunen hielt uns wie bezaubert. Es war mir, als fühlte ich unmittelbar das praesens numen."[7]

He advanced into the very heart of Switzerland, crossed the St. Gotthard and the wildest glaciers,[8] and, as he reaches at sunset an

1 Feb. 7, 1778.   4 Oct. 9, 1776.
2 Letter to Puletchen, June 14, 1773.   5 Schaffhausen, June 7, 1775.   7 Janssen, I, 273.
3 May 21, 1775.   6 Letter to Christian, Nov. 11, 1787.   8 Janssen, I, 48.

island in the Lake of Bienne, he exclaims: ".Welch eine Insel! Ganz Natur! und welche Natur!"[1]

Stolberg's letters show that he is thoroughly imbued with the new spirit. The ocean, the mountain, the torrent, the primeval forest—in a word, the grand and majestic in nature—appeal to him. He lives in that close sympathy with nature which, as will be presently seen, is most characteristic of the author of "Werther."

Herder's and Stolberg's letters show that these authors are capable of an imaginative communion with nature. This feeling is still more perceptible in the correspondence of the young GOETHE, who thinks of himself as a part of nature whose every change affects him too. In winter, it seems to him "als wenn der Winter seiner Natur einerley Epoque haben sollte,"[2] and in autumn he cannot stay in the city, "der Morgen ist so herrlich und seine Seele so ruhig."[3] Again he is in a gloomy mood and writes: "Es regnet draussen und drinne, und die garstigen Winde vom Abend rascheln in den Rebblättern vorm Fenster."[4] As he travels one day at dusk in the region of the Lorraine mountains and the river Saar, his soul feels in perfect accord with his surroundings; "Wie ich so rechter Hand über die grüne Tiefe hinaussah und der Fluss in der Dämmerung so graulich und still floss und linker Hand die schwere Finsterniss des Buchenwaldes vom Berg über mich herabhing, wie um die dunklen Felsen durch's Gebüsch die leuchtenden Vögelchen still und geheimnissvoll zogen; da wurd's in meinem Herzen so still wie in der Gegend."[5] Just as profound is the impression that a landscape near Frankfurt makes upon him. He is returning to the city at night, deeply moved by the scene he witnesses. "Nun muss ich dir sagen," he writes to Kestner,[6] "das ist immer eine Sympathie für meine Seele wenn die Sonne lang hinunter ist und die Nacht von Morgen herauf nach Nord und Süd um sich gegriffen hat, und nur noch ein dämmernder Kreis von Abend heraufleuchtet. . . . . Auf der Brücke hielt ich still. Die düstre Stadt zu beiden Seiten, der still leuchtende Horizont, der Wiederschein im Fluss machte einen köstlichen Eindruck in meine Seele den ich mit beiden Armen umfasste."[7] He loves to stand on this bridge at night and watch the water rushing by, and to have the "liebe trübe Mond" greet him in friendly fashion.[8] Here is a strong and genuine love of nature, no longer the trifling spirit of Anacreontics.

---

[1] Letter to his sister, Basel, Oct. 7, 1775.   [3] Nov. 6, 1772.   [5] June 27, 1771.

[2] Feb. 14, 1769.   [4] Bernays, Der j. Goethe, I, 249.   [6] Dec. 25, 1772.

[7] Cf. also letter to Mamsell F., Oct. 14, 1770.   [8] Jan. 28, 1773.

Goethe's fondness for skating and consequent delight in winter are well known.[1] Most graphically he writes to Johanna Fahlmer: "Heut war Eis Hochzeittag! Es musste gehn, es krachte, und bog sich, und quoll, und finaliter brachs."[2] His joy knows no bounds when Jack Frost arrives: he thinks of the happy hours of outdoor pleasure, as he says to Helene Jacobi: "Eine mächtige Kälte zieht durchs Fenster bis hierher an mein Herz zu tausendfacher Ergötzung."[3] It thaws, and then it freezes again, and he cries jubilantly: "Halleluja! Amen!" —Once he compares life to a sleighride; it is "prächtig und klingelnd, aber eben so wenig fürs Herz, als es für Augen und Ohren viel ist."[4]

The letters of Goethe give adequate expression to the new spirit. The feeling is near that here at last a man has arisen who voices the sentiments of his fellow-beings with consummate skill.

In general it may be said that the letters previous to 1750 have little to do with nature, those after 1750 much. This year is the turning-point, because it was in the summer of 1750 that Klopstock and Sulzer visited the Alps and expressed in their letters a genuine, though not over-enthusiastic, appreciation of Alpine scenery. Of equal importance was Herder's voyage from Riga to Nantes in 1769. The ocean, which had been almost totally ignored or disliked, now received its due recognition at the hands of Herder and, a little later, Stolberg. But, above all, the feeling that man was but a part of nature, and that the closest bonds of sympathy united the two, found its fullest expression in the letters of Goethe.

[1] Cf. Der j. G., I, 348, 374. [2] Jan., 1774. [3] Feb., 1774.
[4] Oct. 14, 1770.—Cf., for Goethe's nature-sense in his letters, W. Barewicz, Goethes Naturgefühl, 7 ff.

IV.

TRAVELS.

IT has been pointed out (Reynolds, *Treatment of Nature in English Poetry*, 193) that books of travel which appeared in England in the eighteenth century dealt usually with such subjects as antiquities, curiosities, laws, manners, customs, but that in the last quarter of the century many scattered descriptions of the natural scenes visited are found. This holds true of Germany, also, but the transition to the new attitude toward nature did not occur "ohne jede Vermittlung" (Winter, 37), as will presently be seen.

One of the early books of travel in the eighteenth century is Martin Wintergerst von Memmingen, *22jährige Reysen durch Europam*, etc. (Frankfurt and Leipzig, 1713). He speaks chiefly of his adventures, sea-storms, and the customs and manners of the people; with only here and there a sentence to reveal his conception of a beautiful landscape. On his way from Rome to Venice he says: "Ich hatte guten Weg, das schönste ebene Land" (87). In another place: "So dann hatte es in dieser Gegend einen überaus schönen Prospect, indeme fast in einem jeden Garten . . . . ein prachtiges Hauss stund" (124). And in winter: "Es hatte nunmehro der Hefftige Frost die See mit einem eysenen Harnisch bekleidet und der Schnee die schwartzen Felder allenthalben weiss überzogen" (183).[1]

In 1723 there appeared Auli Apronii (i. e., Adam Ebert's) *Reise-Beschreibung von Villa Franca Der Chur Brandenburg Durch Teutschland, Holland*, etc. This book differs from Wintergerst's in that it mentions mountains in several places, speaking of the Alps, of course, as terrible, and the Pyrenees (from Toulouse to Montpellier) "so gar nicht so erschrecklich wie die Alpen von Lion aus nach Turin" (198). The mountains about Marsilia (he says) are more difficult to climb than the Riesengebirge (which seemed to him "denkwürdig und . . . . mit seinem Gipfel die Wolcken unter sich läst," 2); and, when one reaches the top, "hat man die Wolcken umb sich und leidet nicht wenig Frost." "In höchst entsetzliche Klippen gelanget man zwar, aber

---

[1] Cf. also 207: "Berg Löwenschantz (der) . . . . der Gegend hilfft ein Ansehen machen."

dergestalt, dass der Pilgrim mit Andacht und Reverentz bald über-
fallen wird" (221).[1] On his arrival at St. Malo the starry sky astounds
him greatly; he observes that it is different from the German, and
adds : "Die Praesentation war unvergleichlich ; so auch nochmahls im
Golfo de Leon und von Cajeta nach Palermo mit höchstem Reverentz
wahrgenommen " (164, 193). He knew the difficulties encountered in
ascending Mt. Vesuvius ; "allein weil er einmahl hier, so wolte er sich
nicht lumpen lassen . . . . stieg auf Vesuvius bis er die Gluth sahe . . . .
kam des Abends spath wieder nach Neapolis, williger nimmermehr dahin
wieder zu kommen, oder die Hecatomben, Puzzolo, Cuma & andere
Löcher wieder zu sehen, als Neapolis so geschwinde zu verlassen "
(389, 393).

In the three following books we note very few references to nature :
Nemeitz, *Nachrichten von Italien* (1726), *Eines gewesenen Römischen
Priesters Reise durch Frankreich & Italien* (1729), *Des Weyland Durchl.
Printzens Maximilian Emanuels Hertzogs in Würtemberg etc. Reisen
durch Teutschland, etc.* (1730). The first says about the city of Trident
(15): "Ohngeachtet des sehr hohen Gebürges & tieffen Thäler, so
stellet die Gegend auf dieser Seiten eine so angenehme Landschaft
vor, als sie kein Mahler ingenieuser mahlen kann," and in another
place he speaks of the "gähen und steiligten Berge " (19) and the
"übel und gefährliche Weg über die Apenninische Gebürge " (363).
The second book has a similar remark on p. 159, and the third mentions "den beschwehrlichen, und zumalen bey so kalter Winters-Zeit
so verdriesslich als gefährlichen Thüringer-Wald " (13 ff.).

Even the poet Haller does not observe much more on his travels
through Germany, Holland, and England, in the years 1723 to 1727.
When he passes the Falls of the Rhine he simply notes in his diary
(6): "Kame den grossen Fall bey finstrer Nacht vorbey." He enjoys
traveling by moonlight (68), considers the country about Hannover
unusually beautiful, but complains of the intensely cold morning air.
Corn and wheat fields he admires above all else (22, 68), and "kleine
sacht angehende Hügel " he mentions near Halberstadt (74). The
ocean, the roar of which one can hear distinctly half a mile away, is a
picture of endlessness, and a terrible sight to unaccustomed eyes (49).
Throughout his journey Haller's interest is centered in cities and
buildings, peoples and their customs, with only an occasional mention
of natural scenery.

[1] P. 403: "Ausser der Stadt Palermo liegen allenthalben Gebürge, aber auch schöne Gärte," he adds
significantly.

One of the best-known travels in the first half of the eighteenth century is Johann Georg Keyszler's *Neueste Reisen* (*1729–31*) *durch Deutschland, Böhmen etc.* He frequently tells something about the countries through which he passes, and describes his favorite landscape in these words (735): "Ich werde mich jederzeit mit Vergnügen der schönen Aussicht, deren man zwischen Fondi und Iteri geniesst, erinnern. Rechter Hand des Weges zeigete sich ein mit Kohl, Flachs und Getraide bebauetes Land, zwischen welchen die Weinstöcke alleenweise, und also dass sich ihr Laubwerk oben mit einander verbindet, angeleget sind. Dieser Prospect endiget sich mit der See. . . . . Linker Hand des Weges sieht man wiederum Weinwachs, Oel & Maulbeerbäume, grosse Cypressen, schöne Pomeranzwäldchen & endlich ein kleines Gebirge."[1] The river Aar and the waterfall of the Velino he describes at length (160, 882). The beauties of the Tyrol, however, he fails to appreciate, for he says: "Von Lindau bis an Tirol trifft man wenige schöne Gegenden mehr an, sondern meistentheils ungleiches Land, viele Waldung & üble Wege" (18). He places it (in a frequently quoted passage)[2] on a par with the Lüneburgian heath (1010).

In *Des Herrn Tiscals Calvisii zu Stendal Beschreibung seiner nach dem Hartz vorgenommen Reisse 1738* there are at least two passages deserving of mention here. From Rothenburg "ist nun die schöne von dem Herrn von Rohr gerühmete Aussicht, da man unter sich in einen tieffen, finstern & greulichen Thal schauet, über demselben weg aber die schönste & angenehmste Landschaft gleichsam en perspective erblicket" (24), and the region about Ilefeld "ist sehr lustig wegen der herum liegenden Gebürge" (36).[3] Interest in the Hartz mountains is certainly on the increase, for eight years later Johann Georg Sulzer[4] recommends a walking tour in these mountains. "Gosslar liegt an dem Oberharz, dichte an den schönsten Bergen. . . . . Gegen Abend reisten wir aus Gosslar nach Clausthal. Der Weg dahin geht immer über die Harzgebirge und ist wegen der schönen Aussichten sehr angenehm, insonderheit für einen, der stark genug ist, den meisten Weg zu Fusse zu thun."

Georg von Fürst (*Curieuse Reisen durch Europa 1739*) and Zacharias Conrad von Uffenbach (*Merkwürdige Reisen durch Niedersachsen etc.*, 1753) offer nothing new as regards the treatment of

---

[1] Cf. also 8, 117, 743, 1005, 1268, et passim.   [2] Friedländer, 13; Winter, 3; Biese, 329.
[3] Cf. also 56, 62.—See the writer's article in Mod. Lang. Notes, XVI, 244 ff.
[4] *Einige Beobachtungen welche ich auf einer Reise von Magdeburg nach dem Oberharz gemacht*, published 1781 in Johann Bernoulli's *Sammlung kurzer Reisebeschreibungen.*

nature, except that they mention the sea. The one speaks of "die gewaltige Macht des Meeres, welches uns so sehr erschröcket hatte" (39), and the other, going from Harwich to Holland, sees a sunrise on the sea: "Sie erschien allmählich an dem Horizont, stieg aber nicht, wie die Poeten fabulirten, aus der See in die Höhe. Doch sahe es artig aus, wie erstlich die Hellung & Strahlen, & nachgehends die Sonne erschien" (III, 257).

About the year 1750 a change in the attitude toward nature may be noted. Up to this time only stray sentences in the books of travel reveal what little attention was paid to the external world. The *Travels* which will be examined presently show a closer observation of nature, interest in some of the phenomena hitherto neglected, and capability of describing landscapes as actually seen.

One of the earliest of this class is Johann Heinrich Lambert's [1] *Beschreibung der Aussicht der Gegenden um Chur* (Bernoulli's *Sammlung*). It was written in August, 1752, according to its editor, who, it may be said in passing, considered it of very little importance. Lambert describes the country about Chur in these words (II, 59): "Zur Seiten der Stadt begiebt man sich auf eine Anhöhe . . . . woselbst ein bewunderungsvoller Anblick der allertreflichsten Vorwürfen unsere Augen entzündet. Aus dunkler Ferne scheinet der Rheinfluss auf breiter Fläche versilberte Wellen gegen uns herzuströmen. Auf beiden Seiten ziehet sich eine Reihe sich schmälender Berge in die Weite. Eine andere Reihe umkränzet sie und lässt hinter sich den gewölbten Bau azurner Lüfte erblicken. . . . . Dort zur Rechten stellt sich unserm erstaunten Gesichte ein Gebirg, ein Fels von ungeheurer Grösse dar. Die Gewölke liegen auf seinen verbreiteten Schultern, und sein Haupt . . . . schimmert bei schwüler Sommerhitze von frostigem Schnee, der die heissen Sonnenstrahlen unerwärmt in die beschatteten Thäler weit von sich herabwirft." He mentions the golden cornfields, the happy mowers at work, the sound of the huntsman's horn, and ends by saying: "Sehet hier die Hügel, die mit Traubengeländern umhangen; dort Berge, so mit Wäldern umkrönet . . . . o des seeligen Aufenthalts! O könnte ich, so wie ihr, beglückte Bewohner, an euerem Glücke, an euerem Vergügen nur einen geringen Antheil haben!"

The next book of importance is Johann Peter Willebrandt's *Historische Berichte und Practische Anmerkungen auf Reisen in Deutschland*, etc. (1758). Not only does he pay more attention to natural scenery, but he is not filled with terror at the sight of mountains or the ocean.

---

[1] Cf. Peschel, Geschichte der Erdkunde, 751.

Quite the contrary. "Das Herz hat in mir gehüpfet," he says (157), "da ich von einem Berge nahe vor Dieppe die offenbare See . . . . entdecket habe. . . . . Ich wenigstens weiss keinen angenehmeren Anblick, als diesen." Near Salzburg he is close to the "Tyrolischen Alpen, deren erstaunlich hohe Gipfel mit Schnee beständig bedeckt geblieben. Es ist dieser Anblick grässlich schön, insbesondere bey heiterer Sommer-Witterung" (332). But his favorite landscape he finds on the way from Palemaille to Blanckennese: "Die Gegenden auf diesem Wege, da man um Nienstäden bald durch die Lage und Kunst schön gemachte Gartens, bald kornreiche Felder, bald schattigte Hölzungen, allezeit aber von einer erstaunlichen Höhe, nicht nur die breite und schiffreiche Elbe, sondern auch an jener Seite der Elbe viele Insuln und das Lüneburger Land übersiehet, auch zu Blanckennese Gebürge, wie die Alpen, erblicket; alles dieses sind wahrhaftig Meisterstücke der Natur" (58).[1]

The growing love for nature undefiled by human hand is emphasized in two accounts found in Bernoulli's "Sammlung." In one of them (*Reise durch Ost-Deutschland*, written in 1762) occurs this remark: "Die Spatziergänge im Walde sind natürlich schön; so wie denn überhaupt durch Kunst an diesem Orte nichts verschwendet ist" (II, 90). The author of the other (*Vom Schwarzwalde*, 1767) delights in the primeval forest: "Ein beynahe ununterbrochener Wald bedeckt dieses Gebirge. Der Wald ist unvergleichlich; da kann man recht sehen, wie eine sich selbst überlassene und Jahrhunderte durch verschonte Hölzung aussieht. Keine Verzierungen von Lustwäldchen, Alleen, Berceaux, Cabinetten können in einen Garten erdacht werden, von denen man hier nicht die Originale in ursprünglicher Schönheit findet; vornehmlich ergötzten mich an einigen Orten die tausenderley Gruppirungen der Nadelhölzer, die vom Erdreich bis an die Gipfel die vortreflichsten Pyramiden vorstellen. Es giebt Wildnisse, wo man auf einem undurchdringlichen Klump, in einer unabsehbaren Strecke, hundertley Arten von Bäumen, mit ebenso vielfältigen Grün, in einander verschlungen siehet; dann wieder Partien wo geradstämmige Fichten mit ihren Kronen ein von Säulen getragenes Dach bilden, unter welchen man zwischen denselben auf einen aufgeräumten mit sanften Rasen bedeckten Boden mit Lust spatzieret" (II, 201).

Owing probably to the influence of Rousseau, travelers now began to tour Switzerland for the sake of her natural beauties. One of the first Germans to appreciate the grandeur and beauty of the Alps, and

[1] For other illustrative passages cf. 45, 47, 49, 207, 216, 247.

to leave a record of his impressions, is Hirschfeld, the author of *Briefe über die vornehmsten Merkwürdigkeiten der Schweiz* (1769). By way of introduction he says (5): "Ich kann Ihnen nicht sagen, mit welcher stillen Vergnügsamkeit und Belustigung des Geistes man durch diese Gegenden reiset, und diese Würkungen auf unsre Seele scheinen mir in der That ein nicht geringer Nutzen zu sein." On his way to Solothurn he sees "viele rauhe felsigte Berge, die die Natur aufgeworfen zu haben scheint, um dem Reisenden einen auf eine urchtbare Art ergötzenden Anblick zu geben" (12). He comments on the alpen-glow near Geneva ("die Aussicht ist sonderbar, aber sehr ergötzend," 54), and on the grandeur of glaciers at sunset (123): "Niemals aber kann ein Anblick in der Natur prächtiger sein, als derjenige, den diese Gletscher bei dem Untergange der Sonne geben."[1] On viewing the fall of an avalanche he says: "Dieses war in der That einer der fürchterlichsten, aber zugleich der schönsten Auftritte, die man jemals sehen kann" (210). The awful majesty of the Alps he beholds at the Grinselwald (140): "Hier eröfnet sich auf einmal die ganze fürchterliche Majestät der Schneegebirge; man erschrickt bei diesem Anblicke, und wünscht dieses angenehme Schrecken allen seinen Bekannten mittheilen zu können; und eine stille Bewunderung der Natur, oder vielmehr ihres grossen Urhebers, bemächtigt sich eines jeden Herzens."[2]

From now on the new attitude toward nature is gradually breaking through in the *Travels*, until in the next decade it entirely pervades the accounts of Sulzer and Forster. Before considering these, brief note may be made of three books of travel written previous to 1775. The author of *Beschreibung einer Reise, welche im Jahre 1769 nach der Sierra Morena in Spanien vom Elsass aus unternommen wurde* (pub. 1780) describes the view from Cadiz as follows (40): "Jenseits des Hafens siehet man die ebenen Felder von Andalusien und die Gebirge von Grenada, die den schweizerischen an Höhe wenig nachgeben; also fast mit einem Blicke, einen mit Schiffen wohl besezten Hafen, ebenes Land, grosse Gebirge, die offenbare See, und eine Stadt, die oben einem Garten gleich sieht. Diese Aussicht ist meiner Meinung nach einzig."[3] In P. Hell's[4] *Reise nach Wardoe bei Lappland etc. im Jahre*

---

[1] Cf. also 180: "Die Gletscher [in den Clarideralpen] schimmern mit einer vortrefflich blauen, oder vielmehr seladongrünen Farbe."

[2] See also 121, 204, 207. [4] Cf. Peschel, Geschichte der Erdkunde, 578.

[3] On board a ship during a storm he expresses no fear, but takes time to speak of the turbulent waters: "Aufgethürmte schwarze Wellen, die oben mit einem weissen Schaum bedeckt waren, stürzten von allen Seiten auf das Schiff, und erhoben es aus dem tiefsten Abgrund, um es wieder dahin zurück stürzen zu können" (81).

1769 (pub. 1835) such expressions as "reizendes Hügelland" (104), "rechts vor uns Berge und steile Felsen, eine höchst angenehme Reise" (105), "herrliche Berge" (109), "schöne Berge" (114), recur frequently. More of the new spirit is shown in (Joh. Fr. C. Grimm's) *Bemerkungen eines Reisenden durch Deutschland,* etc., published 1775 in the form of letters, the first letter bearing the date of December 11, 1773. The winter landscape, as seen from the Strassburg cathedral (169), and the coming of spring in France (Abbeville, March 7) and England (London, April 11), are dwelt upon at length and appreciatively. The landscape about Canterbury (Pt. II, 288), Oxford (Pt. III, 114), and other places in England, affords great pleasure to the author, quite in contrast to Adam Ebert's opinion of England fifty years previously, according to which that country is not worth a visit, except for theologians or merchants ; " dann es ist daselbst nichts ausser London zu sehen."— On the Petersberg near Halle Grimm expresses his delight in nature in no ambiguous way: " Man legt sich nehmlich daselbst auf den Rücken hin und sieht rückwärts die Gegenden unter dem Berge an.— O Natur !! Natur !! möchte man ausrufen,— wie schön bist du hier !!" (Pt. IV, 104). Of special interest for our present purpose is his comment on the way from Landshut to Schmiedeberg : "Beym Herabsteigen des Berges kömmt man zuweilen an lichten Stellen durch die das Auge ein Theilchen der Landschaft erblickt, an deren vollen Genuss es sich bald weiden soll. Die Aussicht durch diese Lücken ist furchtbar schön. Zu den Füssen des Wanderers tiefe wilde Abgründe, die weiterhin in fruchtbare Wiesen oder Aecker übergehen, und an denen sich das Riesengebirge in seiner kolossalischen Grösse und in seinem dunklen Gewande emporhebt" (Pt. VI, 170).

Mention has been already made of Sulzer's recommendation of walking tours in the Hartz mountains. Thirty years after the writing of those lines he traveled from Berlin to the countries of southern Europe and published in 1780 his *Tagebuch einer von Berlin nach den mittäglichen Ländern von Europa in den Jahren 1775 & 1776 gethanenen Reise & Rückreise.* This book, and Forster's *Reise um die Welt,* mark the beginning of a new epoch in the history of travel, devoting as much attention, if not more, to natural scenery, including mountains and the ocean, as to the customs and manners of the people, cities, etc. Of the country from Eisenach to Hünefeld Sulzer says : " Der ganze Weg . . . . geht beständig über Berg und Thal, und ist wegen angenehmer Abwechselungen der Aussichten und einzeler gesperrter,

zum Theil recht romantischer Gegenden ungemein ergötzend" (12).
He is particularly enraptured with the Bernese Alps : "Die höchsten
Alpen, die sowohl durch ihre nackten, sich weit über die Wolken
erhebenden kahlen Felsen, als durch andre mit ewigem Schnee
bedeckte Höhen, eine ganz wunderbare Ansicht geben, die gewiss
niemand ohne eine Art von Entzücken sehen kann " (35). The ever-
changing scenery on the road from Toulon to Nice delights him (157),
he can scarce remove his eyes from the romantic spots near this town
(188), and on his way to Menton he writes : "Man kann nicht leicht
etwas seltsamers, erschrecklichers und zugleich schöners in dieser Art
sehen, als diesen Weg. Er geht über hohe, sehr dürre, meistentheils
aus völlig kahlen Felsen bestehende Berge, und so seltsam zwischen
den obersten Gipfeln dieser Berge herum, dass man beständig neue
und seltsame Aussichten vor sich hat " (237). As he proceeds from
Lugano to Bellinzona he notes in his diary: "Der Weg dahin ist
wirklich von romantischer Schönheit, obgleich hier und da etwas
beschwerlich : erst über die hinter Lugano liegenden Hügel, hernach
durch fruchtbare Thäler und Wege von den herrlichsten Kastanien-
bäumen beschattet. . . . . Mir kam es bisweilen an ganz ebenen, mit
hohen und sehr waldigen Bäumen besezten Plätzen vor [wegen des
spitzig zulaufenden Gewölbes], als wenn ich mich in einer sehr grossen
gothischen Kirche befände" (353). He crosses the Devil's Bridge,
and pictures vividly the awful abyss below him : "Das gewaltige
Brausen des Wassers, die schwindelnde Höhe auf der man steht, der
Staubregen, von dem man bedeckt wird, alles dieses zusammen macht
einen wunderbaren Eindruck auf das Gemüth (369). Alle Begriffe
von Macht und Grösse und unwiderstehlicher Gewalt, die man sich
bei Gelegenheit der menschlichen Anstalten gemacht hat, verschwinden
hier wie Wasserblasen " (373). Enough has been quoted from Sulzer's
diary to show that its spirit is entirely modern. The same spirit is
found in his letters, as shown in the preceding chapter.

Georg Forster's *Reise um die Welt in den Jahren 1772 bis 1775* is
the prototype of the *Travels* best exemplified by Humboldt's *Kosmos*.
It may therefore be permitted to quote from it at length, especially as
it is the last book of travels to be treated of. The author does not
fail to observe the phosphorescence of the sea (66): "Kaum wars
Nacht worden, als die See rund um uns her einen grossen, bewun-
drungswürdigen Anblick darbot. So weit wir sehen konnten schien der
ganze Ocean in Feuer zu sein. Jede brechende Welle war an der
Spitze von einem hellen Glanz erleuchtet . . . . und längst den Seiten

des Schiffes verursachte das Anschlagen der Wellen eine feuerhelle
Linie."[1] Forster is certainly one of the first in the history of travels
to appreciate the grandeur of the ocean, for he says (I, 386): "Der
Anblick des Oceans war prächtig und fürchterlich zugleich. Bald
übersahen wir von der Spitze einer breiten, schweren Welle, die uner-
messliche Fläche des Meers in unzählbare tiefe Furchen aufgerissen,
bald zog uns eine brechende Welle mit sich in ein schroffes, fürchterliches Thal herab, indess der Wind von jener Seite schon wieder einen
neuen Wasserberg mit schäumender Spitze herbeiführte und das Schiff
zu bedecken drohte."[2] He sees the beauty of icebergs (101): "Die
untergehende Sonne verschaffte uns heute Abend einen über alle
Maassen herrlichen Anblick, denn sie färbte die Spitzen einer in
Westen liegenden Eisinsel mit funkelndem Golde und theilte der ganzen Masse einen blendenden Purpurglanz mit."[3] It gives him genuine
pleasure to describe wild, romantic scenery. At Dusky Bay he writes
(118): "Zum Nachtisch ergötzte sich das Auge an der vor uns liegenden, wildnissartigen Landschaft, die Salvator Rosa nicht schöner hätte
mahlen können. Sie war ganz im Geschmack dieses Künstlers und
bestand aus Felsen, mit Wäldern gekrönt, deren Alter in die Zeiten
vor der Sündfluth hinauf zu reichen schien, und zwischen welche sich
aller Orten Wasserbäche mit schäumendem Ungestüm herabstürzten."
One of these torrents he describes at length (I, 135)[4] and then gives
us a detailed description of its romantic surroundings: "Zur Linken
dieser herrlichen Scene stiegen schroffe, braune Felsen empor, deren
Gipfel mit überhängendem Buschwerk und Bäumen gekrönt waren.
Zur Rechten lag ein Haufen grosser Steine, den allem Anschein nach
die Gewalt des vom Berge herabkommenden Wassers zusammenge-
thürmt hatte. . . . . Weiterhin liess sich die durchdringend helle
Kehle der Drossel . . . . und der bezaubernde Gesang verschiedner
Baumläufer an allen Seiten hören, und machte die Schönheit dieses
wilden romantischen Flecks vollkommen. . . . . [Wir sahen] an der
einen Seite das feste Land, dessen hohe, mit Schnee bedeckte Berge
bis in die Wolken reichten; an der andern aber begrenzte der unab-
sehlich weite Ocean die Aussicht. Dieser Prospect ist so bewunderns-
würdig gross, dass es der Sprache an Ausdrücken fehlt, die Majestät
und Schönheit desselben der Natur gemäss zu beschreiben." He

[1] Cf. also I, 33.   [2] See also II, 29.

[3] I, 113: "Die Gestalt [der Eisinseln] war mehrentheils sonderbar, und des zertrümmerten Anse-
hens wegen oft malerisch genug." (See also 96.)

[4] Note, too, II, 65: "Eine schöne Cascade stürzte sich vom Gipfel längs der Felsenwand in den
Fluss herab und belebte die sonst schauervolle, finstere und romantischwilde Aussicht."

describes the ideal spot for the melancholiac thus (I, 144) : "Der
ganze See war mit einem dicken Walde umgeben, der aus den grössten
Bäumen bestand, und die Berge rund umher ragten in mancherlei
Gestalten empor. Alles war öde und still. Nirgends vernahm man
einen Laut . . . . keine Pflanze blühte. Kurz die ganze Gegend war
für ernste Melancholie geschaffen."[1] His sensitiveness to color, especially to the tints of clouds at sunset, finds frequent expression (I, 212 ;
II, 5). Likewise his delight in moonlight scenes (II, 161; I, 264) :
"Der Mond schien die ganze Nacht sehr hell. Kein Wölckchen war
zu sehn. Die glatte Fläche der See glänzte wie Silber, und die vor
uns liegende Landschaft sahe so reizend aus, dass man sich kaum
überreden konnte, hier sei etwas mehr als das schöpferische Werk
einer fruchtbaren lachenden Phantasie."

The eighth chapter of Forster's book begins with the famous
description of Tahiti: "Ein Morgen war's ! schöner hat ihn schwer-
lich je ein Dichter beschrieben, an welchem wir die Insel O-Tahiti 2
Meilen vor uns sahen. . . . . Waldgekrönte Berge erhoben ihre stolzen
Gipfel in mancherlei majestätischen Gestalten und glühten bereits im
ersten Morgenstrahl der Sonne . . . . Aus dem Innern des Landes
ragten mancherlei romantisch geformte, steile Berggipfel hervor, davon
besonders der eine auf eine malerisch schöne, aber fürchterliche Weise
überhing." On his second visit to this island he writes enthusiasti-
cally (II, 37) : "Ich, so schwach auch meine Kräfte waren, kroch ebenfalls mit aufs Verdeck, um mich wenigstens an dem Anblicke der
Gegend zu laben. . . . . Den Morgen war ich früh erwacht, und welch
Entzücken gewährte mir da die herrliche Aussicht ! Es war, als hätte
ich die reizende Gegend, die vor mir lag, noch nie gesehen. . . . . Die
Wälder auf den Bergen waren mit frischem Grün bekleidet, das in
mannigfaltigen Farben durcheinander spielte; die kleinen Hügel hie
und da grünten ebenfalls im neuen Frühlingskleide und verschöner-
ten an manchen Orten die reizende Aussicht. Besonders aber prang-
ten die Ebenen mit allem Schmuck der jungen Wiesen. Kurz, alles
erinnerte mich an die Beschreibungen von Calypso's bezauberter
Insel."

Forster is not an admirer of the Regular Garden, which was popu-
lar up to the time of Kent. He says (I, 228) : "Es gab auch in der
That eine Menge von allerhand wilden Arten in diesen Plantagen, die
untereinander in jener schönen Unordnung der Natur aufsprossten,

---

[1] In another place he tells us: " Wir hätten den ganzen Tag in dieser reizenden Einöde zubringen
mögen " (241).

die über das steife Putzwerk kunstlicher Gärten immer unendlich
erhaben ist."¹   A similar thought he expresses in a letter to his wife
(Mainz, April 11, 1788): "Die Aussicht auf die sich die Mainzer so
viel zu gute thun, ist allerdings schön und prächtig, aber romantisch
ist sie durchaus nicht. . . . . Kannst Du glauben, dass . . . . mitten
in dieser aufs äusserste bebauten Gegend die liebe Natur mit ihrer
reizenden Unregelmässigkeit, ihrem kühlen Schatten, raschen Gipfeln,
rieselnden Gewässern gänzlich vermisst wird ?"

In his letters (which will be quoted here, rather than in Chapter III,
because they were written after the time-limit set for this treatise) are
found some further evidences of his nature-sense, i. e., in those letters
which he wrote before the beginning of the French Revolution. Thus
he writes to Soemmering, as only a close observer of nature would
write (Zellerfeld, April 24, 1784): "Auf den gestrigen ungewöhnlich
lauen Abend, wo uns der Mond so freundlich leuchtete, als wüsste er
nichts von unsrem Abschiede, folgte spät in der Nacht ein Gewitter.
Der Morgen war gelind und lachend; alles lebte im Felde; die Anhö-
hen und Aecker glänzten im freundlichen Grün; die Lerche stieg und
sang, und selbst die melancholische Leine, die sich durch das lange Thal
hinschlängelte, hatte ihren Reiz. . . . . Von hier aus [Osterode] stieg
ich ununterbrochen fort his nach Klausthal, durch schöne Tannen-
wälder, wo die schlanken, himmelanstrebenden Tannen sich vom Sturm
hin und her wiegen liessen. Ich wünsche mir keine erhabnere Musik,
als das Sausen in ihren Wipfeln." Of greater interest are the following lines in a letter to Therese Heyne, which recall to mind Stolberg's
'Süsse, heilige, Natur, Lass mich gehn auf deiner Spur!" (Prag, July
25, 1784): "Ich fing an die Natur wieder lieb zu gewinnen, als man
mich auf einen heimlichen Schattenpfade, zwischen bemoosten Felsen,
durch hohe Buchen und Pappeln und schlanke Tannen, längs dem
rieselnden, rauschenden und plätschernden Waldbach hinabwärts
führte. Es schloss sich um mich her, es nahm mich aus dem Gewirr
jener vor mir offen liegenden Welt, es drückte mich innig an den
Busen der Mutter Natur, die hier einsam und dunkel, doch nicht
grauerlich, sondern nur sanft, nur gleichförmig und stillgleitend, nur
süss melancholisch und mittrauernd, das Gegenbild der in dunkeln
Gedanken verwebten Seele war ! O, für jede Art des Schmerzes liegt
im ewigen Mancherlei der Natur ihrer Bildungen irgendwo ein heil-
samer Balsam." — Like Wordsworth, Forster believes that at certain
moments of our life we may be enraptured by "the meanest flower

¹ Cf. also 356.

that blows," for he says in his diary: "Wer es je selbst erfahren hat, welch einen ganz eigenthümlichen Eindruck die Schönheiten der Natur in einem gefühlvollen Herzen hervorbringen, der nur, der kann sich eine Vorstellung machen, wie in dem Augenblick, wenn des Herzens Innerstes sich aufschliesst, jeder sonst noch so unerhebliche Gegenstand interessant werden und durch unnennbare Empfindungen uns beglücken kann. Dergleichen Augenblicke sind es, wo die blosse Ansicht eines frisch umgepflügten Ackers uns entzückt, [wo wir] . . . . über die verschiedenen Schattirungen des Laubes . . . . [uns] so herzlich, so innig freuen können" (II, 267).

We recognize, then, in Forster, as we did in Sulzer, one of the earliest representatives of the new attitude toward nature. He appreciates romantic scenery, mountains, and ocean, observes the color of the clouds at sunset, delights in dense forests undefiled by human hand, and shows himself capable of an imaginative communion with nature.

On the whole, travelers are hostile or indifferent to nature at the beginning of the eighteenth century, observe her with greater interest and grow more friendly toward her about the middle, and at the end of the third quarter show as much sympathy for her — even her romantic aspects — as do the poets of the same period, except that they do not equal the latter in power of adequate expression.

NOTE. — After this chapter had been written, Oertel's monograph *Die Naturschilderung bei den deutschen geographischen Reisebeschreibern des 18. Jahrhunderts* (Leipzig, 1899) came to hand. His point of view and his sources differ from those above given. His treatise will be of value to future editors of histories of geography (such as Peschel's *Geschichte der Erdkunde*), for he says of the nature of his investigation: "Für unsere Darstellung können nur die wissenschaftlich gebildeten Reisenden in Frage kommen" (13). On this account he concerns himself with the scientific rather than the æsthetic observations and comments of travelers, whereas the present study has tried to do the reverse. It is no little satisfaction, however, to learn that conclusions which largely coincide with his have been independently arrived at here. Oertel states that previous to 1750 "Bruchstücke," after that date " Einzelschilderungen," and with the appearance of Forster's accounts (about 1780) "Gesamtbilder" characterize the travels of the eighteenth century. The men of the first period emphasize the utilitarian side of nature, those of the second insist upon exact observation, and the travelers of the third period describe both scientifically and æsthetically (53). The change about 1750 he attributes to the rise of the natural sciences (29), and that about three decades later to the all-pervading influence of Rousseau (51) and those German writers who followed in his footsteps. Exception may be taken to Oertel's estimate of the service that Hacquet rendered to the history of travel. He says of him '(33) : " Er bereiste die Alpen (1778). Die Vielgeschmähten waren demnach entdeckt." It has been seen that Hirschfeld published the results of his tour in the Alps as early as 1769. Again, Oertel says (34): "Es war neu, dass man der ganzen Natur, auch ihren wilden Scenen und nicht nur fruchtharen Bruchstücken, Interesse entgegenbrachte." It is sufficient to call the attention of the reader to the delight that the author of *Vom Schwarzwalde* (1767) took in the primeval forest, and Grimm (*Bemerkungen eines Reisenden,* pub. 1775) in the wild nature of the Riesengebirge.—In conclusion it may be said that Oertel's investigation will probably not render the present writing superfluous, since the *raison d'être* of the two is different.

SUMMARY.

THE almost total lack of first-hand observation and genuine love of nature characteristic of the seventeenth century as a whole grows less marked with the advent of the eighteenth century, when a more accurate knowledge of nature, and a stronger affection for her, become dominant. Whereas the poets of the first period follow their Latin models closely, and are prone to see almost everything with the eyes of these writers, the men of the second period, especially from the middle of the century, go out into nature, observe her many phenomena, and record their impressions in new and adequate forms.

In the seventeenth century, and even far into the eighteenth (cf. the Anacreontics), the glories of morning and day are sung almost exclusively, though Dach, Günther, and Brockes have some intimation of the charms of evening and night. There is no full appreciation of day and night until after the first half of the century, when the literature (Klopstock, Herder, Hölty), letters (Herder, Mlle. Lucius), and travels (Uffenbach, Forster) show unmistakable signs of the new attitude, of which Goethe was to become the best exponent.

In regard to the seasons, it has been seen that spring, treated more or less conventionally by Opitz and his school, received many advocates in the second and third quarters of the century, the most felicitous, perhaps, being Hölty, although it should not be forgotten that long before him Logau and Dach had sung of the month of May in an original and poetic manner. To Brockes belongs the credit of describing, with more or less skill, autumn and winter, disliked up to his time because they were symbolical of dissolution and death. He discovered their charms, and in due time they became the subject of song (Klopstock, Claudius, Stolberg), despite the Anacreontic poets, who persisted in seeing only their disagreeable features. A similar change occurs in the letters of this period. Frau von Gottsched prefers working at her desk to sleigh-riding (1735), but Klopstock enjoys skating from sunrise to sunset (1768). Goethe's delight in autumn and winter is too well known to need further comment.

The sky and its phenomena, barely mentioned in the preceding century, are noted by Brockes. He does not fail to observe the clouds and winds, or the effect of sunlight or moonlight. A description of a thunderstorm such as we find in Klopstock's *Frühlingsfeyer* (1759) is, however, not within his power.   It is quite remarkable that as early as 1722 Elisabeth von Orleans expresses her delight in seeing this phenomenon.   Not until many years later do we find an adequate appreciation of its majesty (Lichtenberg).

The features of the inland scenery of the seventeenth century are the brook, the hill and valley, and the woods.   These obtain in the poems of the Anacreontic school as well.   A genuine love of mountains which, as was formerly believed, Haller's *Alpen* had inspired, is hardly noticeable before Stolberg, and yet in the letters, travels, and fiction we find earlier indications of this feeling.   Thus, Klopstock and Sulzer express their delight at sight of the first Alpine peaks (1750).   The latter had become conscious, some years previously, of the beauty of the Hartz, about which another traveler (Calvisius) had written in 1738.   After the middle of the century the number of travelers who view with delight Alpine scenery is certainly on the increase, influenced no doubt by the descriptions of Rousseau.   In fiction, too, as has perhaps been shown (*Reise auf die Gebürge*, 1761), love for mountain scenery and beautiful prospects is evident.   For a scientific as well as æsthetic appreciation of the Alps Germany must wait, however, till Goethe's journey to Switzerland in 1779.

Sympathy for the ocean is aroused even later than that for mountains.   Conventional references regarding its wildness, fierceness, and consequent danger are strewn through the literature of the period, but not before Herder's voyage to Nantes, and Stolberg's splendid lines, is its grandeur considered.   This holds true also in the letters (cf. Elisabeth von Orleans and Herder), though Klopstock and, somewhat later, Lichtenberg must not be forgotten.   In the travels indications of the new attitude are discernible in Willebrandt (1758), and expressed more fully in Forster's accounts.

The interpretation of plant and animal life also suffers change, as the range becomes wider, observation closer, and expression more adequate.   Conventional similes are supplanted by appropriate vivifications.   The abundant delight, in a general way, in the bright flowers of the garden gives place to a more intimate pleasure in such flowers as the violet and poppy (Brockes, Götz), and to a genuine enthusiasm for strawberries (Herder).   The stereotype conception of the nightingale no longer prevails, but a sincere appreciation of her song and that of the lark becomes more common (Herder).   The cuckoo is now looked upon as the harbinger of spring (Hagedorn).   The indigenous animals, both large and small, are observed and described (Brockes, Gleim), instead of the exotic, as formerly. All this seems but a preparation for the work of a universal genius like Goethe. His æsthetic appreciation was the more perfect, of course, because it was coupled with close scientific observation.

In the age of Opitz, largely influenced by Horace, the pleasures of country life had been sung. As civilization became more complex, the longing for a simpler mode of life grew proportionately more intense. Throughout the first half of the eighteenth century this desire was expressed with more or less sincerity (Haller, the Anacreontics), accompanied often by a disparagement of man's society, as in the case of Kleist ("Ein wahrer Mensch muss fern von Menschen sein"), and often by a sentimental love for the rest and peace in nature, as is evident in Uz, Götz, and others. Especially after the promulgation of Rousseau's ideas, the thought that nature is not only our comforter, but our guide as well, becomes common even to exaggeration ("Stürmer und Dränger"). Here we need but mention as the typical and purest expression of this sentiment Stolberg's lines, "Süsse, heilige Natur . . . ." In the letters of the period the same feeling is expressed, first brief and vague, then clearer and more distinct (Wieland), and ultimately full and adequate (Herder, Hölty). As regards some of the men, the Anacreontics and Klopstock, for example, it may be added that, unlike Rousseau, they enjoy country life and nature best in the company of friends—a view of nature characteristic of the transition stage. In passing one might well recall that in the history of landscape painting a similar evolution had taken place. In the early works of Italian art, for example, interest is centered in man, nature is altogether ignored or receives but scant treatment (Giotto, and even the early Renaissance painters); later man and nature are of equal importance, the latter serving as a background (Tintoretto); then, as she is more closely observed, she occupies more of the canvas, and the human figures dwindle in proportion, until at last they disappear altogether and the era of landscape painting is ushered in (Claude Lorraine, Salvator Rosa, and the Dutch masters). In descriptions of travel, as above shown, the love of nature grows similarly, although the human element is at no time eliminated. About the middle of the century more attention is paid to natural scenery wide and beautiful prospects are sought out and described (Lambert and Willebrandt), nature in her primitive state delights the eye of the traveler (*Vom Schwarzwalde*), and mountains and the ocean, instead of striking terror into the hearts of the travelers (witness the early accounts of Ebert and Haller), are now a topic of discussion and a source of pleasure (Hirschfeld, Sulzer, etc.). The Falls of the Rhine are now appreciated more than ever before (cf. Klopstock and Stolberg, Heinse).

All nature was looked upon as the work of God by most men of the seventeenth and eighteenth centuries, owing, no doubt, to the paramount influence of the Bible. Thus Brockes wrote many verses descriptive of natural phenomena in order to glorify the Creator, as well as show the usefulness of each part in nature. Haller, Hagedorn, and the Anacreontics largely followed him in this respect, and Klopstock, reared in pietistic surroundings, could not but join them. When nature came to be regarded more and more as a companion and friend, this view gave place to another, according to which an all-pervading spirit permeates nature and links each and all together. Goethe's lines in the *Proœmion* bear on this subject :

> Was wär ein Gott, der nur von aussen stiesse,
> Im Kreis das All am Finger laufen liesse !
> Ihm ziemt's die Welt im Innern zu bewegen,
> Natur in Sich, Sich in Natur zu hegen,
> So dass, was in ihm lebt und webt und ist,
> Nie Seine Kraft, nie Seinen Geist vermisst.

Goethe's thought on evolution, that nature progresses systematically and forms but one continuous chain from the lowest to the highest forms of life, is hinted at by previous poets (Uz, Wieland).

In regard to the literary use of nature in the second and third quarters of the eighteenth century: Writers that have merely observed many phenomena, and have indiscriminately versified them without any regard as to their poetic value, do not concern us here (e. g., Brockes). When, however, their descriptions show that a literary purpose was intended, that there exists a relationship between the various parts, and that the poets meant to present artistically composed pictures, due credit for their efforts must be accorded them (e. g., Kleist). Furthermore, the analogies between external nature and man are indicative of the poet's genius and thought. In the idyllic poets, the slowly winding brook is the emblem of life, in the later poets the rushing mountain-torrent serves that purpose (Stolberg). The use of nature in connection with man's joys or sorrows increases in the course of the century. This is best exemplified by the two poets that mark the beginning and the close of the period which has been made the subject of investigation. Günther in his sorrow has the pale moon as companion, and goes to the animals of the forest to associate with them. Goethe's Werther, as he runs through the whole gamut of emotional experience, finds corresponding moods in nature. This close communion with nature, which becomes particularly marked after the middle of the century (Herder, Hölty, Stolberg), seems but a preliminary step to a still higher conception of nature : her existence independently of man. This is again best illustrated in Goethe, and if any one work were to be singled out, it would probably be the poetic gem *Herbstgefühl*.[1]

[1]For an excellent analysis of this poem cf. H. Corvinus, Zeitschrift für Gymnasialwesen, 1890, 309 ff.

BIBLIOGRAPHY.

Allgemeine Deutsche Biographie, herg. durch die histor. Commission bei d. Königl. Akad. d. Wissensch. Leipzig, 1875 ff.

Apronius, Aulus: Reisebeschreibung v. Deutschl. etc. Villa Franca, 1723.

Barewicz, Witold: Goethes Naturgefühl. Progr. d. Gym. zu Drohobyczu, 1897.

Bernays, M.: Der junge Goethe. 3 vols. Leipzig, 1875.

Bernoulli, Joh.: Samml. kurzer Reisebesch. etc. 4 vols. Berlin-Altenburg, 1781.

Beschreibung e. Reise welche i. J. 1769 nach d. Sierra Morena unternommen. Leipzig, 1780.

Biese, Alfred: Die Entwickelung d. Naturgef. i. Mittelalter u. i. der Neuzeit. 2te Ausg. Leipzig, 1892. Zur Gesch. d. Lit. d. Naturgef., Z. f. vergl. Litgesch., VII, XI.

Bodmer, Joh. Jac.: Abhandlung v. d. Wunderbaren i. d. Poesie. Zürich, 1740. Betrachtungen über d. poet. Gemälde d. Dichter, 1741. Critische Briefe, 1746. Gedichte m. I. G. Schultheissens Anm., 1754. Die Noachide in XII Gesängen. Berlin, 1765.

Brandl, A.: Barthold Heinrich Brockes. Innsbruck, 1878.

Breitinger, J. J.: Critische Abhandlung v. d. Natur d. Gleichnisse. Zürich, 1740. Critische Dichtkunst, 1740.

Briefe an das schöne Geschlecht über verschiedene Gegenstände der Natur. Jena, 1770–71.

Briefe an Joh. Heinrich Merck von Goethe etc., herg. v. K. Wagner. Darmstadt, 1835.

Briefe berühmter u. edler Deutschen an Bodmer, herg. v. G. F. Stäudlin. Stuttgart, 1794.

Briefe deut. Gelehrten an d. Herrn Geheimrath Klotz, herg. v. I. I. A. v. Hagen. Halle, 1773.

Briefe deut. Gelehrten. Aus Gleims lit. Nachlass. Zürich, 1804–6.

Briefe, 318—berühmter u. geistreicher Männer u. Frauen. Berlin, 1835.

Briefe, 300 — aus zwei Jahrhunderten, herg. v. Karl v. Holtei. 2 vols. Hannover, 1872.

Brockes, B. H.: Irdisches Vergnügen in Gott. 9 vols. Hamburg, 1739 ff.

Bürger, G. A.: Deut. Nat. Lit., Vol. 78. Briefe, herg. v. A. Strodtmann. Berlin, 1874.

Calvisius, Tiscal: Beschreibung seiner nach d. Hartz vorgenommen Reisse, 1738.

Claudius, Matthias: Sämmtliche Werke. Breslau, 1774.

Corvinus, H.: Goethes Herbstgefühl. Progr. Braunschweig, 1878 (= Zsch. f. Gymnas., 1890, p. 309).

Dach, Simon: Deut. Nat. Lit., Vol. 30.— Goedeke u. Tittmann, Vol. 9.

Danzel, Th. W.: Gottsched und seine Zeit. Leipzig, 1848.

Denis, I. N. C.: Deut. Nat. Lit., Vol, 48.

Deutsche National-Litteratur, herg. v. Joseph Kürschner. Berlin-Stuttgart.

Elisabeth Charlotte v. Orleans : Briefe, herg. v. W. Holland. Lit. Ver. Stuttgart, Vols. 107, 122, 132, 144, 157.

Fleming, Paul: Deut. Nat. Lit., Vol. 28.— Goedeke u. Tittmann, Vol. 2.

Forster, Georg: Sämmtliche Schriften, herg. v. dessen Tochter u. G. G. Gervinus. Leipzig, 1843.

Friedländer, Ludwig : Über die Entstehung u. Entwicklung des Gefühls für das Romantische in der Natur. Leipzig, 1873.

Fürst, Georg v.: Curieuse Reisen durch Europa etc. Sorau, 1739.

Fürst, R.: Die Vorläufer der modernen Novelle i. 18. Jahrh. Halle, 1897.

Gellert, C. F.: Sämmtliche Schriften. Berlin-Leipzig, 1867.— Briefe an Fräulein v. Schönfeld (Dahlener Antiquarius, Theil I). Leipzig, 1861. —Aufgefundene Familienbriefe, herg. v. A. T. Leuchte. Freyberg, 1819.— Briefe nebst einigen damit verwandten Briefen seiner Freunde, herg. v. J. A. Schlegeln u. G. L. Heyern. Leipzig, 1774.— Briefwechsel mit Demoiselle Lucius, herg. v. F. A. Ebert, 1832.—Tagebuch aus d. J. 1761. Leipzig, 1862.— Zwey Briefe v. G. und Rabener. Leipzig-Dresden, 1761.

Gerstenberg, H. W.: Deut. Nat. Lit., Vol. 48.

Gessner, S.: Schriften. 6 Theile. Zürich, 1765–72.— Oeuvres traduits de l'Allemand à Zuric. Chez l'auteur, 1777.— Briefe an V. B. Tscharner, herg. v. R. Hamel. Rostock, 1881.

Gjerset, Knut: Der Einfluss von James Thomson's Jahreszeiten auf d. d. Literatur d. 18. Jahrhunderts. Diss. Heidelberg, 1898.

Gleim, J. W. L.: Sämmtliche Werke, ed. Wilhelm Körte. 7 vols. Halberstadt, 1811.— Briefe d. Herren G. u. Jacobi. Wien, gedruckt bey J. T. E. v. Trattnern, 1769.— Briefwechsel zwischen G. u. Uz. (Bibl. des Lit. Ver. Stuttgart, Vol. 218), herg. v. C. Schüddekopf. Tübingen, 1894.

Goedeke, Karl, u. J. Tittmann : Deutsche Dichter d. 17. Jahrhunderts. 15 vols. Leipzig, 1869–85.

Goethe, J. W. von : Werke. Histor.-krit. Ausgabe. Weimar, 1887 ff.

Gottsched, J. Chr.: Auszüge aus seinem Briefwechsel. See Danzel.

Gottsched, Louise A. V.: Briefe. 3 Theile. Dresden, 1771.

Götz, Joh. Nic.: Vermischte Gedichte, herg. v. K. Ramler. Mannheim, 1785.— Briefe von u. an G., herg. v. C. Schüddekopf. Wolfenbüttel, 1893.

(Grimm, Joh. F. C.): Bemerkungen eines Reisenden durch Deutschland etc. 3 vols. Altenburg, 1775–81.

Grimmelshausen, Hans J. C.: Deut. Nat. Lit., Vols. 33–35.

Gryphius, Andreas: Deut. Nat. Lit., Vol. 29.— Goedeke u. Tittmann, Vol. 4.

Günther, Joh. Chr.: Deut. Nat. Lit., Vol. 38.—Goedeke-Tittmann, Vol. 6.

Hagedorn, Friedrich v.: Poetische Werke, ed. J. J. Eschenburg. Hamburg, 1800.

Haller, Albrecht v.: Bibl. ält. Schrift. d. Schweiz, Vol. I, 3.—Usong. Carlsruhe, 1778.— Fabius u. Cato. Bern u. Göttingen, 1774.— Tagebücher seiner Reise nach Deutschland, Holland u. England, 1723-1727, herg. v. L. Hirzel. Leipzig, 1883.— Tagebuch über Schriftsteller und über sich selbst. 2 Theile. Bern, 1787.

Harsdörffer, Georg: Deut. Nat. Lit., Vol. 27.

Hawrlant, Franz: Horaz als Freund der Natur nach seinen Gedichten. Progr. Landskron, 1895 ff.

Haym, Rud.: Herder nach seinem Leben u. seinen Werken dargestellt. Berlin, 1880–85.

Hehn, Viktor: Gedanken über Goethe. Berlin, 1888.

Heine, Carl: Der Roman in Deutschland von 1774 bis 1778. Halle, 1892.

Heinzelmann, Wilhelm: Goethes Odendichtung aus den Jahren 1772–1782. Erfurt, 1898.

Hell, P.: Reise nach Wardoe bei Lappland 1769. Wien, 1835.

Herbst, Wilhelm: Johann Heinrich Voss. Leipzig, 1872–76.

Herder, Joh. Gottf.: Sämmtliche Werke, herg. v. B. Suphan. Berlin, 1877–93.— Briefwechsel mit Nicolai, herg. v. Otto Hoffmann. Berlin, 1887.—Von u. an H. Ungedruckte Briefe aus H.'s Nachlass, herg. v. H. Düntzer und F. G. v. Herder. Leipzig, 1861.— Briefe an J. G. Hamann, ed. Otto Hoffmann. Berlin, 1889.— Aus H.'s Nachlass, herg. v. H. Düntzer und F. G. v. Herder. 3 vols. Frankfurt a. M., 1857.

Hermes, Joh. Timoth.: Sophiens Reise von Memel nach Sachsen. 10 Theile. Wien, 1787.

Hettner, H.: Literaturgeschichte d. 18. Jahrh. 4te Aufl. Braunschweig, 1894.

Hillebrand, Karl: Zeiten, Völker und Menschen. 2te Auflage. Strassburg, 1892.

Hirschfeld: Briefe über die vornehmsten Merkwürdigkeiten der Schweiz. Leipzig, 1769.

Hofmannswaldau, C. Hofmann v.: Deut. Nat. Lit., Vol. 36.

Hölty, Ludw. H. C.: Gedichte mit Einl. u. Anm. von Karl Halm. Leipzig, 1870.

Jacobi, Joh. Geo.: Sämmtliche Werke. 3 vols. Halberstadt, 1770–74. — Sämmtliche Werke. 2 vols. Zürich, 1809.—Ungedruckte Briefe von und an J, ed. Ernst Martin, Quell. u. Forsch. II. Cf. Gleim.

Janssen, Joh.: Friedrich Leopold Graf zu Stolberg. 2 vols. Freiburg i. B., 1877.

Karsch, Anna Louise: Gedichte, herg. v. ihrer Tochter. Berlin, 1797.

Keiper, Wilhelm: Friedrich Leopold Stolbergs Jugendpoesie. Berlin, 1893.
Keyssler, Joh. Geo.: Neueste Reise durch Deutschland etc. Hannover, 1751.
Kleist, Chr. Ew. v.: Sämmtliche Werke und Briefe, herg. v. W. Körte. 2 vols. Berlin, 1803.—Herg. v. A. Sauer, Berlin (G. Hempel).
Klenze, Camillo v.: Literature on the Nature-Sense, Jour. Germ. Phil., II—Deutsche Gedichte. New York, H. Holt & Co.
Klopstock, Fried. Gottl.: Sämmtliche Werke. 12 vols. Leipzig, 1798–1817.—Leipzig, 1854.—Kl. und seine Freunde, herg. v. Klamer Schmidt. 2 vols. Halberstadt, 1810.—Briefe von und an Kl., herg. v. I. M. Lappenberg. Braunschweig, 1867.
Koch, Max: Geschichte d. deut. Litteratur. Stuttgart, 1895.—Ueber die Beziehungen der englischen Literatur zur deutschen im 18. Jahrh. Leipzig, 1883.
Kretschmann, K. F.: Deut. Nat. Lit., Vol. 48.
Lambert, Joh. Heinr.: Beschreibung d. Aussicht d. Gegenden um Chur 1752. Cf. Bernoulli.
Lange, Sam. Gotth.: Sammlung gelehrter und freundschaftlicher Briefe. 2 vols. Halle, 1769.
Lichtenberg, Geo. Chr.: Vermischte Schriften. 14 vols. Göttingen, 1844–52.
Liscow, Chr. Lud.: Sammlung satyrischer und ernsthafter Schriften. Frankfurt, 1739.
Logau, Fried.: Deut. Nat. Lit., Vol. 28.—Goedeke-Tittmann, Vol. 3.
Lohenstein, Daniel C. v.: Deut. Nat. Lit., Vol. 36.
Maximilian, Emanuel: Reisen und Campagnen. Stuttgart, 1730.
Meister, Leonh.: Sammlung romantischer Briefe. Halberstadt, 1768.—Über Bodmern, nebst Fragmenten aus seinen Briefen. Zürich, 1783.
Meyer, Rich. M.: Goethe. Berlin, 1895.
Moscherosch, Hans M.: Deut. Nat. Lit., Vol. 32.
Mühlpfort, Heinr.: Deut. Nat. Lit., Vol. 36.
Muncker, F.: Klopstock, Gesch. seines Lebens u. s. Schrif. Stuttgart, 1888.
Nemeitz, Joach. Chr.: Nachlese besonderer Nachrichten v. Italien. Leipzig, 1726.
Nicolai, Fried.: Das Leben und die Meinungen des H. Magister Sebaldus Nothanker. 3 vols. Berlin-Stettin, 1773–76.
Oertel, K. O.: Die Naturschilderung bei d. deut. geograph. Reiseschreibern d. 18. Jahrh. Leipzig, 1899.
Olearius, Adam: Deut. Nat. Lit., Vol. 28.
Opitz, Martin: Deut. Nat. Lit., Vol. 27.
Palgrave, Francis T.: Landscape in Poetry from Homer to Tennyson. London, 1897.
Pyra, Jac. I.: Tempel d. guten Geschmacks für d. Deut. (Deutsche Gedichte 1740–46)—Thirsis und Damon freundschaftliche Lieder. Bern, 1743.
Rabener, G. W.: Sämmtliche Schriften. 3 vols. Leipzig, 1777.—Briefe. Leipzig, 1772.

Ramler, Karl W.: Poetische Werke. 2 vols. Berlin, 1800.

Reise auf die Gebürge, die — Eine Erzählung. 1761.

Reise durch Frankreich etc. eines gewesenen Römischen Priester. Altona, 1729.

Reynolds, M.: The Treatment of Nature in English Poetry between Pope and Wordsworth. Diss. Chicago, 1896.

Scherer, W.: Geschichte d. deut. Litteratur. 8te Aufl. Berlin, 1899.

Schirmer, David : Deut. Nat. Lit., Vol. 27.

Schmidt, Erich : Richardson, Rousseau und Goethe. Jena, 1875.

Schmidt, Klamer Eberh. K.: Auserlesene Werke und Leben, herg. v. dessen Sohn. 2 vols. Stuttg. u. Tübingen, 1827–28.

Schnabel, Lud.: Insel Felsenburg. 4 vols. 1748–51.

Spee, Fried.: Deut. Nat. Lit., Vol. 31.—Goedeke-Tittmann, Vol. 13.

Steinhausen, Geo.: Geschichte d. deut. Briefes. Berlin, 1889.

Stolberg, Christian u. Fried. Leop.: Gesammelte Werke. 20 vols. Hamburg, 1827.

Sulzer, Joh. G.: Betrachtungen über Werke der Natur. Berlin, 1745.— Einige Beobachtungen auf einer Reise von Magdeburg nach dem Oberharz, 1746. Cf. Bernoulli.—Tagebuch einer von Berlin nach d. mittäglichen Ländern in d. J. 1775–76 gethanenen Reise. Leipzig, 1780.—Unterredungen über d. Schönheiten in d. Natur. Berlin, 1750.

Thümmel, M. A. v.: Wilhelmine. Deut. Lit. Denkmale d. 18. und 19. Jahrh., NO. 48.

Uffenbach, Z. C. v.: Merkwürdige Reisen durch Niedersachsen etc. 3 vols. Ulm, 1753.

Uz, Joh. P.: Sämmtliche Werke. Reuttlingen, 1777.—Briefe an einen Freund aus d. J. 1753–82, herg. v. A. Henneberger. Leipzig, 1866. Cf. Gleim.

Versuch einer Litteratur der Reisebeschreibungen. Prag, 1793.

Voss, Joh. Heinr.: Sämmtliche Gedichte. 2 vols. Leipzig, 1833.

Wieland, C. M.: Werke. Berlin (G. Hempel).—Ausgewählte Briefe an verschiedene Freunde, 1751–1810. 4 vols. Zürich, 1815.—Auswahl denkwürdiger Briefe, herg. v. Ludw. Wieland. Wien, 1815.

Willebrandt, Joh. P.: Historische Berichte auf Reisen in Deutschland. Frankfurt-Leipzig, 1758.

Winter, Rich.: Beiträge zur Geschichte des Naturgefühls. Harburg. Jahresbericht des Realgymnasiums, 1882–83.

Wintergerst, Martin (von Memmingen): 22jährige Reysen durch Europam etc. Frankfurt-Leipzig, 1713.

Zachariä, Fried. Wilh.: Poetische Schriften. 4 vols. Braunschweig, 1763–65.

Zesen, Philipp v.: Deut. Nat. Lit., Vol, 27.

Zigler, Heinr. Anselm v.: Deut. Nat. Lit., Vol. 37.